to Want to Be Rich

Finger-wagging moralizers say the love of money is the root of all evil. They assume that making a lot of money requires exploiting others, and that the best way to wash off the resulting stain is to give a lot of it away.

In *Why It's OK to Want to Be Rich*, Jason Brennan shows that the moralizers have it backwards. He argues that, in general, the more money you make, the more you already do for others, and that even an average wage earner is productively "giving back" to society just by doing her job. In addition, wealth liberates us to have the best chance of leading a life that's authentically our own.

Brennan also demonstrates how money-based societies create nicer, more trustworthy, and more cooperative citizens. And in another chapter that takes on the new historians of capitalism, Brennan argues that wealthy nations became wealthy because of their healthy institutions, not from their horrific histories of slavery or colonialism.

While writing that the more money one has, the more one should help others, Brennan also notes that we weren't born into a perpetual debt to society. It's OK to get rich and it's OK to enjoy being rich, too.

Key Features

- Shows how the desire to become wealthy in an open and fair market helps maximize cooperation and lessens the chance of violence and war.
- Argues that it is much easier for the average for-profit business to add value to the world than it is for the average non-profit.
- Demonstrates that the kinds of virtues (e.g., conscientiousness, thoughtfulness, hard work) that lead to desirable personal and civic states (e.g., happy marriages, stable families, engaged citizens) also make people richer.
- Argues that living in small clans for most of their history has given humans a negative attitude towards anyone acquiring more than her "fair share," an attitude that's ill-suited for our market-driven, globally connected world.
- In a final, provocative chapter, maintains that ideal economic growth is infinite.

Jason Brennan is the Robert J. and Elizabeth Flanagan Family Professor of Strategy, Economics, Ethics, and Public Policy at the McDonough School of Business, Georgetown University, USA. He is the author of 14 books, including *In Defense of Openness* (2018) and *Why Not Capitalism?* (2014).

Why It's OK: The Ethics and Aesthetics of How We Live

Philosophers often build cogent arguments for unpopular positions. Recent examples include cases against marriage and pregnancy, for treating animals as our equals, and dismissing some popular art as aesthetically inferior. What philosophers have done less often is to offer compelling arguments for widespread and established human behavior, like getting married, having children, eating animals, and going to the movies. But if one role for philosophy is to help us reflect on our lives and build sound justifications for our beliefs and actions, it seems odd that philosophers would neglect arguments for the lifestyles most people—including many philosophers—actually lead. Unfortunately, philosophers' inattention to normalcy has meant that the ways of life that define our modern societies have gone largely without defense, even as whole literatures have emerged to condemn them.

Why It's OK: The Ethics and Aesthetics of How We Live seeks to remedy that. It's a series of books that provides accessible, sound, and often new and creative arguments for widespread ethical and aesthetic values. Made up of short volumes that assume no previous knowledge of philosophy from the reader, the series recognizes that philosophy is just as important for understanding what we already believe as it is for criticizing the status quo. The series isn't meant to make us complacent about what we value; rather, it helps and challenges us to think more deeply about the values that give our daily lives meaning.

Titles in Series

Why It's OK to Want to Be Rich

Jason Brennan

Why It's OK to Be of Two Minds

Jennifer Church

Why It's OK to Ignore Politics

Christopher Freiman

Why It's OK to Make Bad Choices

William Glod

Selected Forthcoming Titles:

Why It's OK to Get Married

Christie J. Hartley

Why It's OK to Love Bad Movies

Matthew Strohl

Why It's OK to Eat Meat

Dan C. Shahar

Why It's OK to Mind Your Own Business

Justin Tosi and Brandon Warmke

Why It's OK to Be Fat

Rekha Nath

Why It's OK to Be a Moral Failure

Robert Talisse

Why It's OK to Have Bad Grammar and Spelling

Jessica Flanigan

For further information about this series, please visit: www.routledge.com/Why-Its-OK/book-series/WIOK

JASON BRENNAN

Why It's OK

to Want to Be Rich

NEW YORK AND LONDON

First published 2021
by Routledge
52 Vanderbilt Avenue, New York, NY 10017

and by Routledge
2 Park Square, Milton Park, Abingdon, Oxon, OX14 4RN

Routledge is an imprint of the Taylor & Francis Group, an informa business

© 2021 Taylor & Francis

Library of Congress Cataloging-in-Publication Data
A catalog record for this book has been requested

ISBN: 978-1-138-38901-4 (hbk)
ISBN: 978-1-138-38902-1 (pbk)
ISBN: 978-1-003-03225-0 (ebk)

Typeset in Joanna MT Pro and DIN pro
by Apex CoVantage, LLC

Contents

One

Americans have split personality disorder when it comes to money. Everyone wants to get rich, yet everyone is somewhat ashamed of that desire. We admire the rich, but also believe the rich are amoral, vicious people. We enjoy luxury, but also believe that enjoying luxury goods is crass and base. We love material wealth but also denigrate materialism. Many of us signal our wealth whenever we can, but we find it annoying when others do so. We love rags-to-riches stories, but also love stories about noble peasants living the simple life or about rich people getting cut down. We read get-rich-quick books, but no one thinks money is chicken soup for the soul. We nod in agreement when Gordon Gekko says, "Greed is . . . good; greed is right," but then clap with approval when that greedy bastard goes to jail.

You probably want more money. If you had the winning Powerball ticket in your hands, you wouldn't tear it up, nor would you hand it over to the nearest homeless beggar. If your boss offered you a 20% raise, you wouldn't say, "No, thanks, I've got what I need." If your small business—let's say, selling St. Paul the Apostle T-shirts[1]—suddenly doubled its profits, you'd probably think God blessed you rather than cursed you. Even if you don't always express it, you want more money. You sure wouldn't mind being rich.

Hey, same here. I'm just like you. Years ago, I chose to accept a business school professorship because business schools pay their faculty twice as much as liberal arts departments.[2] I admit twice the cash hasn't made me twice as happy. But I've been "poor" (by American standards) and I've been rich, and rich is better.

Still, most of us feel in our guts that there's something unsavory about *wanting* to acquire wealth. The American Dream involves striking it rich—or at least rich enough not to worry about money. Yet, throughout US history, we've been suspicious of wealthy people. Wanting money, wanting to be rich, and indeed, having wealth, seems degenerate. We are not supposed to talk about making or having money in polite conversation.

Wanting more money is sort of like watching pornography. Most people do it,[3] yet most people also feel ashamed of it.

Most Americans are Christian.[4] Jesus says, "It will be hard for one who is rich to enter the kingdom of heaven . . . it is easier for a camel to pass through the eye of a needle than for one who is rich to enter the kingdom of God."[5] Read out of context—which is how most people read this—it sounds like being rich is damnable.

At the same time, many Americans now subscribe to the idea of the "prosperity Gospel." They hold that if they have sufficient faith in God, God will deliver them not just basic financial security, but riches. Baptist minister Russell Conwell claimed,

> Money is power, and you ought to be reasonably ambitious to have it. You ought because you can do more good with it than you could without it. Money printed your Bible, money builds your churches, money sends your missionaries, and money pays your preachers, and you

would not have many of them, either, if you did not pay them. I am always willing that my church should raise my salary, because the church that pays the largest salary always raises it the easiest. You never knew an exception to it in your life. The man who gets the largest salary can do the most good with the power that is furnished to him. Of course he can if his spirit be right to use it for what it is given to him.[6]

Even today, you can turn on your TV Sunday morning and find preachers pushing the same line. Love God and God will provide . . . not just a house, but a big house; not just a car, but a luxury car. It's hard to see why God would provide all those riches if riches ruin our souls. Again, Americans have a split personality disorder when it comes to riches and wealth.

In general, many of the great moralists of history sure seemed to distrust money and wealth. Jesus told us the meek shall inherit the earth and warns us that money corrupts our souls. The King James Bible refers to money as "filthy lucre" four times.[7] While the Buddha was fairly practical about the need for money, he nevertheless lived as an ascetic. Contemporary Buddhist monks try to transcend the need for money.[8] The message seems to be that we would ideally overcome the need and desire for wealth. The philosopher Jean-Jacques Rousseau claimed that the invention of private property was a huge mistake.[9] He thought the love of money makes us vain and stupid, leading to "destructive and narcissistic forms of self-love."[10] Philosopher Arthur Schopenhauer warned us that, "Riches . . . are like sea-water; the more you drink the thirstier you become."[11] Karl Marx predicted that one day the poor would rise up and murder all the rich people and afterward create egalitarian heaven on earth.

Paul McCartney crooned, "Money can't buy me love"—but apparently $48.6 million can buy him a divorce.[12] Occupy Wall Street and Bernie Sanders railed against the 1%—never mind that Sanders is himself now among that 1%.[13] Kansas's old hit song "Dust in the Wind" reminds us "all your money won't another minute buy." Everyone says, "You can't take it with you when you die."

This book is called *It's OK to Want to Be Rich*. I think the finger-wagging moralists have it wrong—or at least have exaggerated their case. Money is the greatest of all human inventions. Loving money, wanting more stuff, and wanting to be rich isn't just normal, but perfectly reasonable. These desires needn't and don't usually debase you or make you a bad person. If you despise money and making money, the problem is usually that you don't understand what money is, what it does for us, and what it takes to make it.

The stoic philosopher Seneca had it right: A well-adjusted person neither scorns luxury nor is consumed by it. Seneca says instead, "It is the sign of an unstable mind not to be able to endure riches."[14] If your money causes you problems, the problem is you, not the money.

I plan to examine—and refute—three widely shared prejudices against money and riches:

1. *It's bad to want money.* Wanting money is crass materialism. It shows a lack of concern for the good things in life. The good things in life are free, and money's a distraction.
2. *It's bad to make money.* Profit-making is exploitative profiteering. For-profit money-making means harming and taking advantage of others. The good vocations selflessly serve others. Not-for-profit is better than for-profit. Business is dirty, and the only thing that vindicates making money

through for-profit ventures is if you give away most of what you make.

3. *It's bad to keep money.* If you do strike it rich, you have a duty to give most of it away. You should live simply so that others may simply live. It's wrong to live high while people die. You must *give back* to society, not merely *take.*

These are indeed prejudices, not just mistakes. These anti-money, anti-market views are based on unfair stereotypes, built-in biases, or prescientific theories of how economies, trade, and money actually work.

I will argue, on the contrary:

1. *It's OK to want money.* Money is freedom. Money insulates us from the bad things in life and makes it easier to lead a life that is authentically ours. It's reasonable to want money because it's reasonable to want what money does for you.

2. *It's OK to make money.* In general, the more money you make, the more you do for others and the more you serve society. Making money can be and usually is a way of serving society. Making money can be and usually is a good and noble thing. The average business or wage earner has already "given back" just by performing their core service. Anything extra is, well, *extra.*

3. *It's OK to keep your money.* Sure, we all have a duty to help others in need. The more we have, the stronger that duty and the more we should help. But investing money in profitable enterprises can in itself be a way of helping, which often does more good long term than most charitable giving. We have the prerogative to enjoy our money too; we aren't born into perpetual debt to society.

I'm not saying the other side is entirely wrong, though. There are indeed people who find no joy in money, or who are shackled rather than liberated by their money. There are plenty of rich people who got rich through ignoble means; their wealth is to be condemned. Many of us, both rich and middle class, give far less to charity than we should. But none of that vindicates our general distrust of money or the wealthy.

Pretty much everyone loves money. But hardly anyone loves money for its own sake. They love what money can do: open doors, send us places, show us new opportunities, remove sources of worry, and buy us security against most of the bad things life sends our way. They love that money can liberate us to have the best chance of leading a life that's authentically our own, of being the authors of our own lives. They love that money puts them in a position to care for others rather than needing care from others.

They are not rapacious and greedy. Still, they want more rather than less, and frequently want more than they have. They want to live in comfort and indulge in some luxuries.

And that is OK.

EVERYBODY HATES THE RICH

You can see the US's split personality disorder in our attitudes toward the rich. We love *People* magazine. Entrepreneurs such as Steve Jobs, Elon Musk, and Mark Cuban fascinate us. But we also sneer at the rich and tend to assume they're bad people. (Some of them, such as Steve Jobs, were.[15])

As psychologist Adam Waytz explains in *Scientific American*,

> The main problem with rich people and ethics, has nothing to do with them per se; it has to do with us, and

the fairly well-developed stereotypes we hold about what the ethics of the rich are. Unlike, say, people who repair laundry machines, or Aleut musicians, or female cricketers (about whom we do not hold well established stereotypes) we have a fairly consistent view of the rich, and it is not good. We perceive the rich to be untrustworthy and cold to the point where we even take joy in their misfortunes (such as when a businessman gets soaked by a taxi driving through a puddle—admit it, you laughed). Rich people elicit jealousy and envy, and not the type that leads us to aspire to be more like them.[16]

He's not kidding. Some psychologists have run experiments measuring when we feel good or bad about others' misfortune. It turns out we delight in the misfortunes of the rich.[17] We stereotype rich people as being highly competent but cold.[18] The phrase "Rich people are evil" returns 65,000 hits on Google; "Rich people are good" only about 600.

Waytz says most people tend to assume that rich people are less ethical. Studies that claim the rich are indeed less empathetic and more callous make national news headlines.[19] We enjoy reading studies that support what we already believe: the rich are jerks. But most of these studies-gone-viral have serious methodological flaws. In fact, there isn't good evidence the rich are worse than others.[20] No one posts that to Facebook.

EVERYONE THINKS PROFIT IS BAD

You have two basic ways to get more money: make it or steal it. Many people think those are really the same thing. Even in the supposedly liberal capitalist United States, people believe that "for profit" = "evil."

In a famous paper, researchers Amit Bhattacharjee, Jason Dana, and Jonathan Baron find that most Americans subscribe to what they call "anti-profit beliefs." That is, most Americans believe that profit-seeking "is necessarily in conflict with beneficial outcomes for consumers and society."[21]

Now, both philosophers and economists have long argued that you cannot judge actions or policies based on people's intentions. The mother who reads pseudoscientific gobbledygook and then refuses to vaccinate her kids *means well*. She genuinely intends to help her children, but she still harms them. Her intentions are good but her actions are bad. On the other hand, suppose your heart surgeon is a sociopath. All he cares about is fame and money. Still, when he saves your life, he does something good, even though his intentions were self-serving.

As I'll explain in the next chapter, for-profit business activity is responsible for a gigantic, thirty-fold increase in human welfare over the past few hundred years. Nevertheless, it appears that the average person, ignorant of economics and world history, uses a simple heuristic: If something is done *for profit*, it must be harmful; if it is done *not for profit*, it must be good.

To test for anti-profit beliefs, Bhattacharjee, Dana, and Baron first provided experimental subjects a list of familiar Fortune 500 firms. They told subjects each firms' rate of profit. They then asked subjects to evaluate 1) whether society is better off with or without that firm existing, 2) whether they think the firm deserved its profits, 3) whether the profits came at the expense of others or not, 4) whether the profits result from a lack of competition, and 5) whether the people running the business have good or evil motives.

The results: subjects generally assumed profit is bad. The more profit a firm makes, the more subjects assumed—without any evidence, mind you—that the firm harms society and that society would be better off without it. The more profitable a firm is, the more subjects assumed—without evidence—that the business must have unethical business practices, doesn't deserve its money, benefits from monopoly, and that its managers must have evil motives.

Bhattacherjee, Dana, and Baron then compared their experimental subjects' ratings of firms to the firms' ratings on the Domini Social Index, a corporate social responsibility index which evaluates companies' social, environmental, and employment practices. The index isn't perfect, but it's at least one widely used and trusted measure of business ethicality and positive impact. Subjects in the study tended to assume that more profitable companies must have worse business ethics. However, the more profitable firms in fact tend to be better rated on the Domini Social Index. Less profitable firms tend to have lower social index scores.

Bhattacherjee, Dana, and Baron didn't stop there. Other experiments showed that subjects assumed that the more profit an entire industry makes, the more harmful the industry must be, and the worse business ethics that industry as a whole must practice.

They ran an experiment in which they had subjects consider four hypothetical business activities. They had half of the subjects imagine the firms in question are not-for-profit, and half imagine the firms are for-profit. Otherwise, the description of the firms is exactly the same. They then asked subjects whether they thought the firms are harmful or beneficial to society. Even though the subjects had no evidence for their conclusions, most subjects automatically concluded that the for-profit organizations are harmful and the not-for-profit organizations are socially beneficial. Again, by experimental design, subjects had no information, evidence, or reason to reach such conclusions. The available information about the firms was the same. So, their evaluations reflected pure bias.

Finally, Bhattacherjee and his co-authors ran an experiment in which they described hypothetical businesses that planned to adopt either ethical or unethical business practices. They asked subjects to estimate how profitable the hypothetical companies would be. Subjects estimated that the companies with bad business practices would make lots of money, while the companies with good business ethics would make less.

In short, what these studies showed is that nearly everyone in the US, conservatives and liberals alike, is biased against money-making. They presume, without evidence, that the more profitable a company is, the more it harms rather than helps society, the more unethical its practices must be, and that its leaders' motives must be evil. They presume that choosing to adopt bad business ethics will lead to higher profit, while choosing good business ethics practices will reduce profit. They automatically assume that not-for-profit firms are beneficial for society.[22] In short: most Americans believe profitability is bad.

MONEY MEANS DIRTY

Everyone wants money, but Westerners also regard money as profane.

Money is not just a medium of exchange. As political theorist Michael Sandel says, "markets don't only allocate goods; they also express . . . certain attitudes toward the goods being exchanged."[23] In his bestselling book *What Money Can't Buy*, and in his high-cost, for-profit speeches, Sandel continually complains that putting a market price on certain things—sex, kidneys, naming rights for sports stadiums, certain forms of life insurance—is inherently disrespectful. Philosopher David Archard complains that buying blood for blood banks ruins the social significance of giving blood: "the meaning of non-market exchanges would have been contaminated by the existence of the market exchanges. The monetary value which the latter attributes to any good exchanged would have 'leaked into' the former and changed its meaning."[24] Philosopher Elizabeth Anderson objects to surrogacy services—in which an infertile couple hires a woman to carry a fetus for them—on the grounds that commodifying "women's labor" necessarily signals disrespect for women.[25]

Each of these philosophers agree that putting something for sale communicates something, and what it communicates isn't nice. They think putting a price on something isn't compatible with seeing that thing as having value as an end in itself or having sacred value.

Their basic argument is simple. Money has no value in itself. It's just useful in the way a hammer is useful. So when you put a price on something, you are—they think—expressing that the thing in question has the same kind of value as money. If you charge $1000 for saving a life, you're saying saving a life—a holy, sacred value—is the equivalent of a thousand dollar bills—things with profane, merely instrumental value. Therefore, putting a price on things is incompatible with seeing them as sacred or being valuable as ends in themselves. Or so they say.

What these complaints share is a certain theory of the social meaning of money. It turns out that Westerners view monetary transactions, and money itself, as impersonal, instrumental, and selfish. As Terence Mitchell and Amy Mickel summarize, "In the conventional economic perspective, money is viewed as a utilitarian commodity that is ordinary, mundane, impersonal, and neutral. It is profane, with only quantitative meanings."[26] Sociologists Maurice Bloch and Jonathan Perry concur: "The problem seems to be that for us money signifies a sphere of 'economic' relationships which are inherently impersonal, transitory, amoral and calculating."[27]

Note that Mitchell, Mickel, Bloch, and Perry are not endorsing this view of the meaning of money. They aren't arguing that money is in fact bad or has a bad meaning. Rather, they intend to report that this is the meaning that most Westerners impute onto money. However, it turns out, this conception of the meaning is not universal. Other cultures (and even Westerners at other times) do not impose this negative, dirty meaning onto money. For some cultures, putting a price on something is in fact the way you signal that it has sacred meaning.[28] But Americans think money is dirty. Many people find even routine market transactions repugnant.[29]

No surprise, then, that it turns out Westerners also believe money has a corrupting influence. They believe that introducing money into relationships will "crowd out" altruism and virtue, and instead make people nastier, less kind, and more selfish. (In fact, the empirical research actually tends to show the opposite effect—money makes us nicer.[30])

YOU ALREADY ARE RICH

Why does any of this matter? Does it matter whether it's OK to get rich?

One reason to care is that we have an interesting intellectual puzzle. Americans—and most other Westerners—have contradictory attitudes. We want money but think wanting money is bad. We admire but also vilify the rich. We believe the free enterprise system made America great and the West rich, but we also assume for-profit business is harmful and evil.

So, as a culture, we have a schizophrenic, split personality. As individuals, we have incoherent and incompatible beliefs. Something's got to give. We need to resolve the contradiction—and the best way to do that, I'll argue, is to eliminate our anti-money, anti-market, anti-profit, and anti-rich prejudices.

But there's another reason. It matters whether we regard the desire for more money, the desire to make money, and the desire to keep money as good or bad. With the tools of the social sciences, we can determine when such desires lead to good or bad outcomes for all. In fact, as I'll explain over the next few chapters, in a properly functioning market system, the way you can make money for yourself is by creating value for other people. Markets translate our desire for personal wealth into socially beneficial outcomes. But if most people don't understand that—and, guess what, they don't—this will cause them to bite the hand that feeds them and kill the goose that lays the golden egg. It will cause them to vote for regulatory political regimes that actually make it *easier* to make money through harmful, socially destructive means. It will cause them to scorn businesspeople and encourage young people to work in what are in fact less valuable but, to untrained ears, nic-er-sounding careers. If we continue to think it's not OK to want money, to make it, or to keep it, we'll end up voting against our own interests. A society in which people think farming is sinful is a society where people go hungry. We better make sure moral views reflect economic evidence.[31]

But there's yet another reason: When I say "rich people," you picture Jeff Bezos or Oprah Winfrey. But you should also picture *yourself*. If you are a typical person living in the West today, then you are not only one of the richest people alive today. You are one of the very richest people to have ever lived. You enjoy wealth and luxuries that previous generations wouldn't think possible.

Historically, almost everyone everywhere was dirt poor and on the verge of economic starvation. Almost everyone throughout history lived in what the UN would now call "extreme poverty." Economist Angus Maddison estimates that as of 1 AD, the total gross domestic product (GDP) per capita—economic production per person per year—was only about $457 USD in 1990 dollars. By 1820, it was only $712 USD worldwide.[32] In today's dollars, adjusting for inflation and the cost of living, that means the average person in 1820 lived on only $1350 a year. And that's just the average. In fact, because of income inequality, most people were even poorer than that.

On most reliable estimates, per capita world product—the total amount of yearly economic production per person—just barely doubled between 5000 BC and 1800 AD.[33] Since then, it has increased by a factor of at least 30.[34] Importantly, wealth has been created, not just moved around. The US by itself in 2018 produced—in real terms—almost 300% of the entire world's economic output in 1950, and something like 80–100 times the entire world's economic output in 1000 AD.[35] We are swimming in riches our ancestors could scarcely imagine.

An American living today at what the US government considers the "poverty line" has a standard of living around three times that of the average American in 1900 AD.[36] What we call poor today in the US entails a better standard of living than what we considered middle class 100 years ago. Even left-leaning economist Paul Krugman wrote in 1996,

> most families in 1950 had a material standard of living no better than that of today's poor or near-poor . . . it does

not seem at all absurd to say that the material standard of living of the poverty-level family in 1996 is as good as or better than that of the median family in 1950.[37]

In a rigorous paper examining American consumption over time, economist Bruce Sacerdote finds that Americans today enjoy a lot more stuff than they did in the past. Since 1960, American households below the median income—that is, in the bottom 50% of income—have gone from owning 0.5 to 1.5 cars on average. (And, despite what grandpa says when he gets a few beers in him, today's cars are far more reliable, safe, powerful, and efficient than the cars of 1960.) Only about 75% of bottom-income households had indoor plumbing in 1960; now they all do. The number of bedrooms and bathrooms per household has also gone up, even among the poorer households, and even though the number of people per household has gone down since 1960.[38] People have more space today than in the past.

What if we look just at the material goods that so-called "poor" households in the US possess, say by looking only at households making $20,000 a year or less? As of 2005 AD, 73.4% of Americans living at the official poverty line owned at least one car or truck, while 30.8% owned two or more cars or trucks.[39] According to the US Census Bureau's Annual Housing Survey, as of 2017, basically all poor households had electricity, heat, a refrigerator, oven, microwave, and stove. About 90% of poor households had air conditioning in their home. Half had an electric dishwasher. Two-thirds had a washing machine and clothes dryer. If we confine our attention just to the very poorest households, those making less than $10,000, the numbers don't change.[40]

According to the US Energy Information Administration's Residential Energy Consumption Survey, nearly all poor households ($20,000 in income or less) own LCD, plasma, LED, or projection TVs. At least half have a cellphone, and half have at least one smartphone. More than half own a computer.[41]

The US Census Bureau's Survey of Income and Program Participation examines, among other things, patterns of food consumption and food deprivation. It finds that only about 6% of poor households report "sometimes" not having enough food, while about 1.5% report "often" not having enough food.[42] Amazingly, in 2009, during the Great Recession, it found fewer than 1 in 5 poor households, and only about 1 in 25 poor children, experienced even one single instance of reduced food intake over the past year due to a lack of money.[43]

I wish things were even better than that, but these are amazing numbers. It used to be that the poor went hungry most of the time, and many died of starvation and starvation-related diseases. Poverty isn't what it used to be.

The United States considers the poverty line for a single adult living alone in 2018 to be about $12,000. If we adjust for the cost of living, so that we're comparing apples to apples, this puts this "poor" American around the top 15% of income-earners in the world today.[44] Indeed, it only takes about $36,000/year in income for an American to be among the top 1% of income-earners worldwide.[45]

So, before you say "Eat the Rich," remember, you are the rich. And that means all those worries I described above—all those biases against rich people and money-making—apply to you. Asking whether it's OK to want money, to make it, and to keep it isn't some abstract philosophical exercise. It's not about Lori Greiner and Daymond John. Rather, we're asking whether you and I are bad people, a bane to society. We're asking whether rich people like you and me should stop living high while people die and instead give it all away. We're asking whether you and I should feel proud or ashamed of ourselves and what we do for a living.

I don't think so. In general, wanting money, making money, and keeping it is OK.

Two

> [T]he gross national product does not allow for the health of our children, the quality of their education or the joy of their play. It does not include the beauty of our poetry or the strength of our marriages, the intelligence of our public debate or the integrity of our public officials. It measures neither our wit nor our courage, neither our wisdom nor our learning, neither our compassion nor our devotion to our country, it measures every-thing in short, except that which makes life worthwhile
>
> —Robert Kennedy, 1968[1]

In the quotation above, Senator and US Attorney General Robert Kennedy has a point, even if his reasons for stating this point were less than noble.[2]

GDP is indeed an imperfect way of measuring economic activity or economic well-being. Simon Kuznets—the very economist who developed the modern concept—made clear its limitations and also warned against using it as a stand-in for welfare. People who bash GDP likely don't realize that they are repeating the very criticisms the person who invented the concept offered.

GDP measures when a housecleaner vacuums my house or when a babysitter watches my kids; it doesn't measure when I do that same work for myself. It measures every government dollar spent but doesn't account for government waste. It doesn't measure the things you enjoy without spending extra money, such as long walks on the beach or browsing the Internet. It measures cigarettes smoked, bombs exploded, and prisoners housed, but it doesn't measure joy, love, friendship, or freedom. It's thus tempting to conclude, as Bobby Kennedy advises, that focusing on GDP growth is focusing on the wrong thing.

By extension, it's easy to conclude that wanting wealth distracts us from the good things in life. Money can buy you a Rolex and a Porsche, but it cannot buy you real self-esteem or the esteem of others. It can buy marijuana and oxycodone, but it cannot buy you elation and joy. It can buy sex, but it cannot buy love. Perhaps—as Bobby Kennedy's dad showed us—it goes a long way in helping buy a presidency and seats in the senate, but it cannot buy actual honor. The best things in life cannot be bought. So, why not stop chasing money and instead focus on what really matters?

At first glance, these are all reasonable worries. But let's instead take a long look at what happens when people—and entire countries—have lots of money, and when they don't. Let's see what money—and the real wealth it represents—actually does to people and does for them. Once we take a long look, we'll see money is a wonderful, liberating tool. Money is *essential* for enabling human beings to work and cooperate together on a mass scale.

MAKE A LIST

Let's start with an exercise. Make a list of four different kinds of goods or services you can buy. Don't include basic necessities—the bare minimum food, water, shelter, and medicine you need to live—on this list.

1. *A good or service you love that genuinely enriches your life.* For instance, is there a good or service you have or tend to buy which, if you're honest with yourself, makes your life better than that of many of your friends and loved ones?
2. *A good or service you buy that you could do without.* You like it, but you could go without it without much loss.
3. *A good or service you want, but you wish you didn't want.* You desire it, but you also desire *not to desire* it. Your life would be better if you didn't want the thing in question.

For instance, for me, the list might be:

1. My Kiesel Vader guitar and Mesa/Boogie JP2C amplifier. I've played guitar since middle school. I can afford high-end gear. I notice and appreciate the high quality. Playing guitar and bass, whether in a band or by myself, is one of the most satisfying things I can do.
2. Most of the restaurants I eat at. I'm not a foodie. I don't really appreciate fine foods the way some people do. We're more "I don't feel like cooking tonight" than "Let's see what's in the Michelin Guide" restaurant people.
3. Chocolate. If I didn't crave chocolate, it sure would be easier to stay in shape.

What's your list?

Part of my point is that if your money isn't making you happy, maybe you're not spending it the right way. You should spend more of it on list 1 items and less of it on list two and three items. With a little more conscientiousness, we can make our money work more toward our happiness. (For instance, new research shows that one of the best ways to make your money serve you is to use it to *save time.*[3])

Money is good if you spend it wisely. Saying money is bad is like saying glue is bad. Glue is great when you use it for good things, such as repairing a broken vase or building a model airplane. It's bad when you huff it to get high.[4]

But my bigger point here is that consumption is not all the same thing. When people complain about loving filthy lucre, they have in mind items on the second or third list. They forget that some of our consumption brings real meaning and joy to our lives. They're forgetting that much of the real meaning and joy we find in life—the kind we have nothing to be ashamed of—comes from or is mediated by consuming *goods*.

EXPRESS YOURSELF/COME TOGETHER

Look around any mall, airport, public park, or college campus, and you'll notice that people choose to advertise the brands they enjoy. The kid on the skateboard wears a Flip T-shirt. The guy with the grey pony tail has a Gibson guitar shirt. The middle-aged professional wears a Nike golf shirt. People want you to know which sports teams they endorse, what their hobbies are, what their politics are, and where they went to school. We pay companies money for the right to turn ourselves into walking billboards. Social activist Naomi Klein and the fine people at Adbusters find this behavior infuriating. Nevertheless, Adbusters.org also sells Adbusters-branded T-shirts and coffee mugs, so you can signal to others through your consumption that you're above branding.

We're not just slaves to trends. We're not merely trying to signal our wealth and status. That's part of it, but our behavior is more interesting than that.

Instead, we each have a self-image. We want other people to share our image of ourselves. We want others to know where we come from, who we are, what we care about, what we're proud of, what we oppose, and what we do. Brands are a kind of language; they allow us to communicate with each other. By wearing a Metallica T-shirt, I'm a little less anonymous as I walk through the crowd.

Brands work hard to cultivate an image, a social meaning to their products and services. Apple communicates edgy, artsy, and cool. BMW communicates exciting, while Mercedes communicates refined. Product Red communicates concern for social justice. And so on. Sure, companies work to construct these images to get our money. But that we willingly display their logos shows that we want them to do it. They construct a social meaning for their brands, which we then use to construct our own public image.

Beyond that, common consumption can bring us together. You might have friends you met because of a shared hobby. Wearing a Marshall Amplification T-shirt at my son's soccer practice led to me joining two different bands. I've made real-life, in-person friends I met through online forums for high-gain tube amp enthusiasts. Our consumption can bring us together.

HEDONIC ADAPTATION

People in the West live today with unprecedented freedom. Unlike people in previous generations, we may pretty much decide as we please where to live, what to do for a living, whether to live a traditional or nontraditional lifestyle, and what kind of people we will be. Yet as we've thrown off economic, cultural, and political shackles, people do not seem to bask in their liberation but instead have become more aware of their internal shackles—their anxieties and neuroses.[5]

Consider the day you buy a new phone. New car. New house. Take the first bite of a long-awaited meal. Receive an acceptance letter to your first-choice university. Fall in love. Get engaged. Get married. Hold your newborn child for the first time. You may feel ecstatic. But the feeling fades away. We are not free, it seems, to continue to be happy with our past successes. Things that were sources of elation cease to thrill us after a while.

There is some evidence that we are walking on what psychologists call a hedonic treadmill. The idea is that individuals have a baseline level of happiness. Your baseline might be different from mine. Good things give us a temporary boost; bad things a temporary cut. But over time, we tend to revert back to our baseline.

I don't want to overstate that—many studies find that certain life events have lasting effects.[6] Still, we're all familiar first-hand with how the pile of presents on Christmas morning loses its excitement by New Year's Day. If so, then we might reasonably wonder: Even if we're wealthier today than before, are we any happier? Even if average Americans are in the top 1% of world income, is this money doing them any good?

THE END OF THE EASTERLIN PARADOX

It's easy to study whether wealth makes people taller. We break out the rulers and measure height. It's harder to study whether it makes them happier. What "happiness" means is hotly debated. Is it personal flourishing? Psychological contentment? A feeling of joy or pleasure? Further, we don't have a ruler to measure people's happiness. We cannot, say, point a hedonometer at your brain and say, "Ah, right now you're experiencing 96.3 degrees of happiness."

At best, what we can do is ask people to rate how happy they are (overall or at some given point in time) on some scale, perhaps first training them to understand what the scale means with the hope of getting consistency between subjects. But, of course, that's an imperfect measurement device. People might be self-deceived. Certain cultures' norms—against bragging or against whining—might pressure people to answer in dishonest ways.

Starting in 1974 and through subsequent work, the economist Greg Easterlin argued, on the basis of such survey data, that money cannot buy happiness. What he seemed to find was that while richer people are generally happier than poorer people, the *absolute level* of wealth didn't matter. In a richer country, the person making $100,000 a year is generally happier than the person making $50,000. In a poorer country, the person making $20,000 is generally happier than the person making $10,000. But, his evidence seemed to show, the person making $100,000 in the rich country is not much happier than the person making $20,000 in the poor country. Being comparatively richer than your neighbors makes you happy, but the actual level of income doesn't.[7]

What Easterlin seemed to find was that after people had enough money to meet their basic needs and ensure some basic security, the relationship between money and happiness plateaued. Note carefully: Easterlin wasn't making the common sense claim that each additional dollar buys you less happiness—that an extra dollar is usually worth more to a poor person than a rich person. Economists call that "diminishing marginal returns." Rather, Easterlin was saying that once people around the world make around $12,000–$15,000 in today's dollars, additional money doesn't have any further positive effect on their happiness. This result is called "the Easterlin Paradox."

The Easterlin Paradox was the conventional wisdom for a long time, though it always had plenty of critics. But in 2008, economists Betsey Stevenson and Justin Wolfers offered a powerful challenge which appears to have refuted Easterlin's findings.[8] As Nobel Laureate Daniel Kahneman summarizes their results:

> The most dramatic result is that when the entire range of human living standards is considered, the effects of income on a measure of life satisfaction (the "ladder of life") are not small at all. We had thought income effects are small because we were looking within countries. The GDP differences between countries are enormous, and highly predictive of differences in life satisfaction. In a sample of over 130,000 people from 126 countries, the correlation between the life satisfaction of individuals and the GDP of the country in which they live was over .40—an exceptionally high value in social science. Humans everywhere, from Norway to Sierra Leone, apparently evaluate their life by a common standard of material prosperity, which changes as GDP increases. The implied conclusion, that citizens of different countries do not adapt to their level of prosperity, flies against everything we thought we knew ten years ago. We have been wrong and now we know it.[9]

Betsey Stevenson and Justin Wolfers found that around the world, the richer a country is in absolute terms, the happier its people tend to be. Contra Easterlin, it's not just about being richer than one's neighbor. Rather, the typical person in a rich country is happier than the typical person in a poor country. Around the world, the person making $100,000 a year tends to be happier than a person making $20,000 a year. Sure, money exhibits diminishing returns. But money has a pretty big effect. As Wolfers elaborates, differences in income

> can explain why people in Burundi are at 3.5/10 on a happiness scale, and Americans are at 8/10. My interpretation is that big gaps in happiness are easily explained by big gaps in income. So why do we interpret things differently?[10]

Interestingly, Stevenson and Wolfers do not simply find a strong correlation and large effect size between money and happiness. They also find that richer people and people from rich countries are more likely to say they feel loved and respected, less likely to say they feel sad or depressed, more likely to say they laughed or smiled in the previous day, and more likely to say they were able to choose how they spent their time in the previous day.[11]

Gallup frequently polls Americans, asking people to rate themselves as very happy, fairly happy, or not to happy. The good news is that 42% of poor people with household incomes of, say, $10,000–20,000 reported that they were very happy. But as household incomes rose, the number saying they were very happy approached 100%, while the number saying they were "not too happy" approached 0%.[12]

This kind of survey data may understate just how much money affects our happiness. Economist Tyler Cowen comments, insofar as some studies seem to show that money has only a weak overall effect on happiness, this

> says more about the nature of language than it does about the nature of happiness. To give an example, if you ask the

people of Kenya how happy they are with their health, you'll get a pretty high rate of reported satisfaction, not so different from the rate in the healthier countries, and in fact higher than the reported rate of satisfaction in the United States. The correct conclusion is not that Kenyan hospitals possess hidden virtues or that malaria is absent in Kenya, but rather that Kenyans have recalibrated their use of language to reflect what they reasonably can expect from their daily experiences. In similar fashion, people in less happy situations and less happy societies often attach less ambitious meanings to the claim that they are happy. Evidence based on questionnaires will therefore underrate the happiness of people in wealthier countries.[13]

As a matter of fact, when we ask people to rate their happiness on a scale of 1 to 10, richer people and people in richer countries do circle higher numbers than poor people or people in poorer countries. But if the gap seems smaller than you would suspect, that could be an artifact of our inability to measure happiness directly. Maybe people doing backbreaking labor, with high rates of food insecurity, with little leisure, and with high rates of child mortality are surprisingly resilient and happy. Or, as Cowen suggests, maybe their idea of what constitutes "happy" is less ambitious than what a rich Westerner thinks constitutes happiness. The rich Westerners are happier, but they reserve the word "happy" to reflect an even more exalted state.

At any rate, according to our best available evidence, richer people are indeed happier people. You can't literally buy happiness, but having money makes it far more likely you'll be happy. Why?

Psychologist Abraham Maslow hypothesized that we have a "hierarchy of needs." The items low on the hierarchy—such as maintaining body temperate, having enough air, food, or water—are more urgent, but the items higher—companionship, love, self-fulfillment, self-transcendence—are more meaningful. Nevertheless, we tend to pursue the lower items first, and only pursue the higher items once we've secured the lower. No one worries about finding true love if they're suffocating. People try to ensure that their kids can eat before they worry about finding meaningful and fulfilling hobbies. Money can't quite buy the important things high on the hierarchy. But what it can do is buy the things low on the list, and moreover, ensure that we need not worry about those things. It thus liberates us and gives us a real shot, if not a guarantee, at getting the higher goods.

MONEY IS FREEDOM

The philosopher Isaiah Berlin noted that native English speakers use the word "freedom" to refer to dozens of different things.[14] For instance, we sometimes use the word freedom to refer to the power or capacity to achieve our ends. When we say a bird or Superman are free to fly, we mean that the bird and Superman have the power to fly.

The philosopher G. A. Cohen says that money—or rather the real wealth it represents—is like a general-purpose ticket.[15] The more money you have, the more things you have the power to do.

Want to start a rock band? You need money for instruments. You need money to make time for learning how to play. Want to see the world? You need money for travel. Want to experience fine art? You again need money for travel. Want to enjoy cuisines from around the world? You need money to eat out— or to buy the ingredients and learn to cook it yourself. Want to grow a beautiful garden, or your own food? You need money for tools, seeds, pots, soil, and space.

The point isn't just that everything costs money. The point is that money makes the world accessible. The richer you are, in general, the more you have the capacity to do.

Cohen concludes that to have money is to have an important kind of freedom. The average person today has, compared to her ancestors, more real options available to her about what kind of life she will to lead, whom she will be, and what she will do at any given moment. In this way, at least, people today—the richest cohort of human beings who have ever lived—have significantly more freedom than anyone else who has ever lived.

What does all this new wealth and money buy?

LEISURE

Some anthropologists think that hunter-gatherers had plenty of leisure time. When there are few mouths to feed, plenty of game to hunt, and plenty of land, perhaps it was easy to collect enough food. It seems that the switch to agriculture meant more work. Agricultural communities can feed far more people— though perhaps at first at a lower average rate of health—but farming takes more work than hunting.[16]

The industrial revolution, at first, seemed to exacerbate that trend—people started working even longer hours. Peasants in medieval England engaged in backbreaking labor during planting and harvest season, or when they did forced labor for their lords. But they also seemed to have had plenty of leisure—albeit leisure coupled with extreme poverty—during off-times. When England started to industrialize, this enabled the country to feed even more people, but at least at first, it appears work hours jumped up dramatically.

Fast forward to 1870. In that year, the United States was one of the richest countries in the world in terms of per capita income, and by extension one of the richest countries ever to have existed. GDP per person was around $3000 in current dollars,[17] an astounding number compared to the poverty-stricken past. (Indeed, $3000/person *today*, let alone in 1870, still puts you in the top half of world income earners.[18])

Yet, in 1870s America, the average person started working full-time by age 13 and kept working until he died. That same average person would work about 5000 hours a year, spending about 2000 hours on home chores and 3000 hours on work outside the home for pay. The typical American of 1871—in one of the three richest countries ever to exist by that time—would spend 61% percent of his or her life awake and working. They would enjoy about 99,000 hours of waking leisure time over their lives but spend over 150,000 hours working.[19]

Now fast forward to today. Today, the typical American spends less than 28% of her life awake and working. The average American starts working full-time after age 20 and retires before age 63. They work—whether at home doing chores or outside the home for money—for half the number of hours per year as their predecessors in 1870. They enjoy about 330,000 waking hours of leisure over the course of their lives. That means the typical American today can expect to enjoy over 26 *more years* of waking leisure time than their counterparts right after the Civil War. Keep in mind that this number—26 years—does *not* include time asleep.[20]

Think of what people can do with all that leisure. They might play video games or watch Netflix. They might enjoy Broadway shows or classical music. They might learn an instrument or pick up a hobby. They might volunteer to help others. They might take vacations to Disney World or to some place the travel snobs go. They might do nothing at all. How we spend our leisure time is up to us. Perhaps some of us use our leisure in more meaningful or impressive ways than others. Nevertheless, we have at least two and a half extra decade's worth of waking leisure time over Americans just 140 years ago.

LIFE AND HEALTH

Part of the reason we have more leisure time is that we have more time, period.

In England in 1000 AD, the average life expectancy at birth was only 26 years.[21] In the US in 1900, it was only 43 years at birth.

These numbers are a bit misleading. People did age faster back then, but it's not as though in 1000 AD, 26 made you an old man. Rather, children under age 5 died at such high rates that life expectancy was astonishing low. The year 1800 was the richest year at that point in human history. Yet in 1800, all around the world, at least 30% of children died before age 5 in every country, even in the richest countries like the United States, the Netherlands, or the United Kingdom. In India, the death rate before age 5 was over 50%. Today, around the world, even in the poorest countries, the numbers are far lower. In the US, the Netherlands, the UK, and other rich countries, child mortality is exceedingly rare.[22]

In the year 1800, in the US, if you survived or avoided the childhood diseases and made it to age 5, you might expect to live another 40 to 50 years. But even then, you'd likely die young compared to people today.

Today, we live far longer, thanks mostly to a combination of vaccines, better nutrition, and better sanitation. The streets of New York may have more car exhaust, but they aren't full of

E. coli-containing horse excrement. Our water is clean. Our food is clean. We have vaccines against some diseases, including polio, diphtheria, the measles, and the flu. Smallpox—which may have killed half or more of the Native Americans after European contact—has been eradicated. As a result, we are less likely to get life-threatening illnesses when we are young. Thanks to better nutrition, when we do get sick, we are more likely to survive and recover.

In the rich parts of the world, children no longer suffer stunted growth or mental development from a lack of food. If anything, the "poor" in rich countries like the US are more likely to be *obese* than underweight. Obesity is a real problem, but it used to be the rich person's disease. Greg Easterbrook observes that,

> Four generations ago, the poor were lean as fence posts, their arms bony and faces gaunt. To our recent ancestors, the idea that *even the poor* eat too much might be harder to fathom than a jetliner rising from the runway.[23]

In the West, people can expect to live into their 80s or 90s. It's hard to imagine a greater bonus to our personal freedom—to our ability to lead lives that are authentically our own—than gaining an additional few decades of healthy life.

LIGHT AND BOOKS

Nobel Laureate economist William Nordhaus points out that darkness isn't what it used to be. Today, when the sun goes down, life goes on.

It didn't always. Light used to be incredibly expensive. Even kings—in their vast castles and palaces—lived in the darkness and shadows.

Between the 14th century and today, the cost of light dropped by a factor of 12,000. Yes, 12,000. A typical candle produces about 65 lumen-hours of light. Back in England in the early 1300s, a million lumen-hours of light would have cost your about $50,000 in today's dollars. (Keep in mind that at the time, the average per person income was only about $1000 in today's dollars.) Today, a million lumen-hours of light—the equivalent light of about 15,400 candles—will cost you a few dollars. The price of light dropped gradually between 1300 and 1800. It dropped dramatically between 1800 and 1900. With the spread of electricity, it dropped even more dramatically between 1900 and today.

Think of what that means. Today we enjoy the ritual of reading to our children before bed. In the year 1300, most people wouldn't have been able to afford the light to read. They also could not afford the books and were usually illiterate anyway.

On that point, today there are far more books than ever before. Part of the reason for that is that physical books are now cheap. Thanks to the printing press and advances in printing, the cost of producing a book is less than 1/300th of what it was 700 years ago.[24]

Today you don't even need a printed book. If you have an Internet connection and some sort of computer, smartphone, or tablet, you can get pretty much any old book for free, legally. You can also get pretty much any *new* book for free, illegally, including this one, if you know where to look, though my editor at Routledge asks you please not to look.

SAFETY AND PEACE

If you turn on the news, reporters will tell you about every armed conflict around the world. You might get the wrong impression. In fact, we live in the most peaceful time in history. As psychologist Stephen Pinker notes,

> many intellectuals have embraced the image of peaceable, egalitarian, and ecology-loving natives. But in the past two decades anthropologists have gathered data on life and death in pre-state societies rather than accepting the warm and fuzzy stereotypes. What did they find? In a nutshell: Hobbes was right, Rousseau was wrong.[25]

As far as our best anthropological evidence shows us, hunter-gatherers tended also to be warriors and raiders. As city-states and then nation-states appeared, the human tendency to make war did not disappear. States have the ability to organize warfare on a massive scale. Advances in technology enable warriors to be more lethal. Hunter-gatherers can murder and rape an entire neighboring tribe, but by the end of World War 2, a single bomber could destroy an entire city with one bomb.

Nevertheless, fewer people die in war or armed combat today than in the past. Lawrence Keeley and other archeologists note that in contemporary hunter-gatherer tribes (our best approximation of our past), the percentage of males dying in war and armed conflict can be as high as 60%. Among Europeans in the 20th century, it was just a few percent, despite two devastating World Wars.[26] Today, despite various civil wars, the never-ending war in Afghanistan, and so on, the rate of people dying in armed conflicts is only about 1/100,000, down from about 22/100,000 as of 1950.[27]

Social scientists disagree about just why the death rates from armed conflict are down. But part of it has to be a wealth effect. As people get richer, they have less to gain and more to lose from armed conflict. Think of your typical post-apocalyptic horror movie showing a war of all against all when people are desperate for the remaining resources. Now reverse the trend—imagine instead that resources, riches, wealth, and opportunity become ever *more abundant*. The urge to fight withers away. Wealthy societies make a life of peaceful trade and cooperation more secure and rewarding.

Our wealth makes us not just safer from each other, but safer from the earth itself. The International Disaster Database seems to indicate that the number of weather-related disasters is indeed on the rise, though the data is relatively poor before the 1960s. Nevertheless, even as the climate warms up and the weather gets in some sense worse, the number of deaths from natural disasters is far lower now than even 100 years ago.[28] The main reason is that increased wealth allows people to afford better, safer, and more disaster-resistant housing. It allows governments to buy better infrastructure which helps insulate them from such dangers. It allows people to have the knowledge and ability to flee certain approaching disasters, such as hurricanes.[29]

Further, work and transportation related accidents are down. People are far less likely to be severely injured on the job now than, say, 100 years ago.[30] Part of this is because as we become richer, we turn to less dangerous forms of work. Part of this is that as we become richer, we can afford more safety devices which reduce the danger of the riskier forms of work.

[...] e earth is warming up. We have good reason to thin [...] e will be less hospitable in the future than it is now. Nevertheless, even though the severity of climate-related disasters will be higher in the future than today, our best available economic evidence indicates that most of our descendants will nevertheless be far better off than we are.

William Nordhaus, who won a Nobel Prize for his work on the economics of climate change, asks readers to imagine what would happen if we take no steps to reduce greenhouse gas emissions: "To give an idea of the estimated damages in the uncontrolled (baseline) case, those damages in 2095 are $12 trillion, or 2.8% of global output, for a global temperature increase of 3.4°C above 1900 levels."[31] Nordhaus thus estimates that world product in 2095 will be $450 trillion in 2010 dollars, which means he's assuming about a modest 2.5% annual growth rate. On Nordhaus's estimate, even if we do nothing to reduce climate change, people will be vastly better off in 2095 than they are now. If the world continues to grow at even a conservative 2.5% rate and given the UN's projection that world population will be about 11.2 billion,[32] the average person worldwide by 2095 will be as rich as the average German or Canadian right now.

The 2007 *Stern Review on the Economics of Climate Change* provides far more pessimistic estimates.[33] It argues that by 2100, climate change will reduce economic output by 20%. But this does not mean world product in 2100 will be 20% lower than in 2007. Rather, this means that climate change will reduce world product in 2100 by 20% compared to a hypothetical baseline in which carbon emissions and temperatures had not risen.

Of course, Nordhaus and Stern argue, and I agree, that we should take steps to mitigate climate change. But the point remains that even as economic growth born of industrialization makes the climate worse, it also reduces the harm the climate does to us.

CULTURE—AND ACCESS TO CULTURE

In *The Wealth of Nations*, the founding text of modern economics, Adam Smith said that the division of labor is limited by the size of the market. That applies to cultural products too. There are more people. People live much longer. They have far more money and leisure time to consume cultural products.

What does that mean? As economist Deirdre McCloskey calculates, the world market for culture is about 9000% *bigger* than it was 1000 years ago.[34]

The philosopher Jean-Jacques Rousseau believed that commercial societies teach people to be vain, stupid, manipulative, and preoccupied by trinkets. He didn't present empirical evidence for this conclusion; he just looked out his window and wagged his finger at his neighbors. But it's an interesting hypothesis, even if Rousseau failed to give us any reason to believe it: Maybe the market for culture is bigger, but the culture we produce and consume is perhaps not 9000 times better.

Tyler Cowen—who uses economic analysis to explain the development of art, music, and food—would respond that yes, the bigger market for culture produces Taylor Swift and all the artists you consider vapid. Yes, it creates NASCAR and all the sports and performances you consider base. It produces Snickers bars and all the food you consider philistine. But it also produces all the people you consider geniuses. Mozart, Beethoven, Michelangelo, Shakespeare, and the other "greats" were for-profit businesspeople, after all. Today, the American economy is far more commercial than Rousseau's Geneva was. Yet, a child born to working class parents is far more likely to read Rousseau today than in Rousseau's own time.

It's not a coincidence that in most societies, centers of artistic and cultural development also tend to be centers of trade. After all, trading cities are the places that bring different people with different ideas together. People encounter new ideas, borrow from others, and synthesize their own and others' ideas into new cultural products. It's not a surprise that the center of artistic development in ancient Greece was Athens, not Sparta, or that you have far more culture and art being made in Seoul rather than Pyongyang, or New York City rather than Moscow.[35]

Today, thanks to increased wealth and the technology created by that increased wealth, you have much of the world's culture at the tip of your fingers. Want to listen to a new form of music? In the 1950s, you were at the mercy of the radio and whatever albums you could afford from the limited selection at your local shop. In the 1800s, you could listen to whatever your neighbors could play, if they could play and could afford an instrument. Now, thanks to Spotify and related services, you listen to pretty much anything from anywhere, for free.

CAN BUY ME LOVE?

You cannot literally buy love. But nevertheless, having more money tends to predict having a better marriage.

Psychologist Eli Finkel, author of *The All or Nothing Marriage*, notes that over the past few thousand years, our standards for a good marriage have increased dramatically. In the past, people wanted some companionship and a partner in the division of labor. Now they want emotional support, self-fulfillment, a person they can admire, and a person who aids them in becoming their best selves. That's a tall order, and the higher divorce rates around the Western world in part reflect the fact that we demand more from our marriages than most can reasonably hope to get.[36]

The thing is, the rich have a much better tendency to actually *succeed* in getting all these higher goods out of marriage than the poor. Part of the reason, perhaps, is that the same psychological factors—such as conscientiousness, perseverance, impulse control, emotional intelligence, general intelligence—which contribute to you becoming upper middle or upper class also contribute to making you a good marriage partner. People—especially conscientious people—don't marry at random. Conscientious and thoughtful people tend to marry one another.

But, at the same time, there is good evidence that the money itself makes a difference. Money problems are among the biggest sources of marital stress and strife. Higher incomes tend to insulate people from those stresses. More money, fewer problems. Finkel notes that the divorce rates are much lower for the rich than for the poor, while marital satisfaction rates are much higher for the rich than for the poor. He explains:

> The problem is not that poor people fail to appreciate the importance of marriage, nor is it that poor and wealthy Americans differ in which factors they believe are important in a good marriage. The problem is that the same trends that have exacerbated inequality since 1980—unemployment, juggling multiple jobs and so on—have also made it increasingly difficult for less wealthy Americans to invest the time and other resources needed to sustain a strong marital bond.[37]

In general, in the United States, marriage rates have been going down. But high-income women have seen gains in their rates of marriage, while high-income men have had only a small drop. As Catherine Rampell writes on the New York Times Economix blog, "Marriage is for rich people. . . . Rich men are marrying rich women, creating doubly rich households for them and their children. And the poor are staying poor and alone."[38]

HOW MONEY MAKES MASS COOPERATION POSSIBLE

When we talk about market economies, we often emphasize competition between firms. But while you compete with the few, every time you do anything, you cooperate with unseen millions. At base, an economy is a system of people working together. Human beings are unusually social animals. We work with strangers, on the scale of billions.

Consider a simple object—a number 2 pencil. As journalist Leonard Read points out, literally millions of people worked together to produce that pencil, though perhaps only a few hundred realized that they were doing so. The person who mines the iron that goes into the ball bearings in machines that make the paint that coats the pencil does not know he is helping to make pencils. The professor who taught the engineer who designed the blade on the chainsaw that cut the lumber didn't know that she was helping make a pencil. Millions of disparate people work together to produce even the simplest items. Only a tiny minority even know what they are helping to do.

The process of making a pencil is so complex that—literally—no one on earth knows how to make a pencil from scratch. A single human who tried to do so wouldn't get it done in her lifetime. But something somehow gets these people to work together. Somehow, pencils—and computers and jets—get made.

How? A functioning economy—a functioning system of cooperation—needs three things:

1. Information: Something must signal to individuals what they need to do.
2. Incentives: Something must induce people to act on that information.

3. *Learning*: Something must correct people's mistakes and teach people to become better at responding to information and incentives.

Modern market economies serve these needs with three mechanisms:

1. *Information*: Market prices.
2. *Incentives*: The ability to acquire private property and wealth for one's own disposal, as one sees fit.
3. *Learning*: Profits and losses.

What this means, in short, is that money is the tool that enables human beings to cooperate on the scale of billions. Let me explain.

Even if you've never taken an economics class, you've probably heard that market prices are a function of supply and demand. Market prices are not arbitrary numbers set by capricious managers.[39] The manager at Walmart can place a price sticker on a TV, but she cannot dictate that the TV will actually sell at that price. Instead, market prices emerge as a function of supply and demand.

The forces of supply and demand are in turn determined by all of us, as individuals, acting on our disparate knowledge and disparate desires as we react to the world around us. We each know certain things and want certain things. We each have two basic tendencies. All things equal, as things become absolutely costlier, we tend to stop pursuing them and instead look for substitutes. For instance, if this book cost $100 or $500, fewer people would buy or read it. All things equal, as things become costlier, we are more willing to produce those goods and services ourselves. For instance, if I learned that

Walmart wanted to pay cashiers $1500 an hour, I'd quit my cushy professorship—my dream job!—and work at Walmart instead. The forces of supply and demand are determined by all the choices and trade-offs that every individual in the economy makes, given the information they have.

What this means, then, is that market prices convey information about the relative scarcity of goods in light of people's desire for those goods. Market prices thus tell producers and consumers how to adjust their behavior to other people's wants and needs. And, importantly, they do so without actors in the market needing to understand what prices are. Few people, aside from economists, understand that market prices encapsulate the knowledge and desires of everyone in the market. But people act on the information signal that markets provide, even though they don't know that prices are a signal.

For instance, suppose there's a disaster at tin mines, or that miners are finding it harder and harder to find tin. Suppose at the same time, someone figures out a cheaper, easier way to isolate aluminum from bauxite. Because it's harder to get tin, the price of tin will naturally rise. That's because people will only supply tin if it's profitable to do so, and—in light of the disasters—it will only be profitable at a higher price. At the same time, the price of aluminum will drop. That's because the new process makes it cheaper to make pure aluminum, and so producers can make a profit at a much lower price. (In 1824, the year aluminum was discovered, even though aluminum is the third most common metal in the Earth's crust, it was incredibly expensive to produce pure aluminum. Aluminum was thus treated like a precious metal—that's why there's an aluminum rather than silver or gold cap on the Washington Monument.)

When this happens—when the price of tin rises and the price of aluminum falls—Coca-Cola, Campbell's soup, and others who use them will switch from tin to aluminum. They will thereby conserve the scarcer resource (tin) and instead use the more abundant resource (aluminum). Only the people who really need tin—those who get the most value from using it—will continue to buy it. So the prices will induce everyone to conserve resources, and they will tend to ensure that the resource goes to the highest value user. Coca-Cola and Campbell's soup don't even need to know *why* tin is suddenly expensive and aluminum so cheap. They just need to see the prices, and they'll adjust their behavior accordingly.

Further, in the pursuit of profit, Coca-Cola will also try to find a way to use less aluminum. After all, the less aluminum it uses, the less it has to pay, and the more profit it can make. In fact, for this very reason, soda cans use much less aluminum now than they did 50 years ago. Soda cans now have a curved top and bottom (as opposed to the straight cylinders of 50 years ago) that allows them to be stacked high despite containing less metal. This is not because Coca-Cola executives are environmentalists, but instead because they knew they'd make more profit if they could cut costs. Market prices induce them to *conserve*.

Or, suppose there's a power outage. You'd hate for your chilled wine to get warm, so you rush to the store to buy ice. But when you get to the store, you find the ice is selling for $12 a bag.[40] You'll probably decide it's not worth buying ice for wine. What you don't realize, though, is that by choosing not to buy the ice, you thereby leave it for the diabetic who needs it to cool her insulin.

In a market, there is no *central* planner, no individual person or committee in charge. But that doesn't mean market economies are unplanned. Instead, in the global market economy, there are 7.3 billion planners. Each person on the market has different information about the economy, about local opportunities and costs, and especially about her own wants and desires. For an economic system to function, this diffuse information must be conveyed to all the other individual planners. When economists say that prices are a function of supply and demand, they mean that prices convey this diffuse information to everyone else. In markets, prices are measurements.

I'll spend more time talking about the meaning of profit in the next chapter. But remember from the last chapter that the typical American thinks "profit" is a dirty word—they think profits = exploitation, cheating, social harm. They're right that in special cases—in cases where people genuinely cheat others or game the system—profits do mean that. But they're wrong to think profits generally mean that.

On the contrary, here's how profits work. Let's say you are considering becoming an artist who makes sculptures using smashed up new Macbooks. You buy laptops, smash them to bits, and then reassemble them into Steve Jobs statuettes. Let's say each statuette costs you $100,000 to make. You then offer them on the market.

People will buy your statues only if they think the statues are worth more, to them, than the price they have to pay. In turn, you will only continue selling the statues if you can get more money than the price you had to pay to make them.

Let's say—amazingly—people love your statues, and they're willing to pay $200,000 for each of them. That means most of the buyers value your statues at more than $200,000, and no one who buys them values them at less than that. (They wouldn't buy them otherwise.) So, in this case, you're making $100,000 profit on each statue. (Profit equals revenues minus costs.) At the same time, this means that you *transformed* parts and labor worth $100,000 into something worth $200,000. The very fact that you are making a profit, in this case, proves you are *creating value*, that you are adding value to the world. Profit is your reward for finding a way of taking things people value a certain amount and transforming them into something they value even more. And you can only make a profit so long as you keep doing that, so long as you make *other people* better off.

Let's say—more realistically—no one wants to buy your statuettes for more than $100,000. The most you can get is $10 at flea markets, even though it cost you $100,000 to make each statue. In that case, every time you sell a statuette, you *lose* $99,990. As a result, you don't make a profit, you instead suffer a loss. You'll probably quit making those statuettes. Note, importantly, that the problem is not merely that *you* are losing money. Rather, the losses here—the opposite of profit—means you are making the world worse for others, too. You took something other people valued at a high level and transformed it into something they didn't value much at all. You didn't create value; you instead destroyed value.

In short, the profit/loss mechanism is essential for getting people to create value. Profits reward people for creating value for others. Losses punish people for destroying value.

Remember, an economy needs information, incentives, and learning mechanisms. In market economies, information gets conveyed through market prices, while profit/loss serves as the learning mechanism that corrects people's behavior and gets them to work together better over time. In theory, though, an economy could work with some other mechanisms of information, incentives, and learning.

For instance, inside my own household, my family members can just see firsthand what other people need. We are motivated by love, not by the pursuit of private property. And we can use social rewards and punishments—such as loving or angry words—to correct each other's behavior. We don't run a market inside our four-person household.

But those mechanisms don't work on the scale of 1000, let alone 7.3 billion people. As far as we know, there isn't a way to coordinate a 7.3 billion-person economy except through market prices.

You might think, well, what if we had one person, or a smart committee of economists, just plan the entire economy? But economists discovered in the 20th century that this just won't work. The problem is that the task of planning an entire economy is just too complex for the few to do. If a command economy sets prices, these prices don't measure anything. Artificial, government-mandated prices convey no information about scarcity or demand. Without real prices, planners cannot perform reliable economic calculations. Without a price system, they can't reliably decide whether producing apples or oranges is more productive. How would central planners know whether to use plastic or metal shovels, gold or aluminum wire, leather or canvas in shoes? That would require that one hold in mind a precise inventory of the quantities and qualities of all the different factors of production in the entire system, together with full geographic knowledge and possibilities open to different locations, all at once, and be able to go through all the possible permutations. The simple answer is they don't know. That's why command economies and central planning have never worked. Even the Soviet Union and other purportedly socialist countries ended up having to rely, in various ways, on markets and market prices to make decisions.

WANTING MORE VERSUS WANTING MORE THAN

Once we examine what money and wealth do for us, it makes sense to want more.

However, there's both a good and bad form of wanting more. Consider the difference between these two cases:

1. Jeff wants more wealth, period, in absolute terms.
2. Jeff wants to have more wealth than Kate.

Wanting more in absolute terms can be a good thing. We can all get richer at the same time. Indeed, we have all been getting richer at the same time.

But wanting more than others have is a bad thing. Here, the goal isn't to be better off, period, but to be higher in status and better off than others. This kind of desire can be satisfied only in a competitive way. We can all satisfy the desire to be better off, period, but we cannot all satisfy the desire to be better off than others. Once we stop enjoying what wealth does for us and instead focus on using wealth as a form of status-competition, then we've turned wealth from a liberator to a mechanism of conflict.

If Jeff desires to have more than Kate, he can satisfy that desire by acquiring more stuff while Kate stays the same. But he would also be happy if Kate loses everything while he stays the same.

My point here is to acknowledge that there is a reason to be suspicious of certain kinds of desires for money. But let's clarify what the problem is. The desire to be better off is good. The desire to be *better off than others* is not.

Paul the Apostle—writing over 1800 years before economists understood what money is and does—said the love of money is the root of all evil. He is no doubt correct that excessive greed can corrupt each of our souls. Some people are willing to do almost anything to get more money. As soon as you say, "I'll do anything!"—whether you'd do anything for money, fame, love, or even the good of your church—the "Devil" has you. Fair enough.

But what Paul misses is all the good money—and the real wealth it represents—does. Money is freedom. Money buys us peace, safety, opportunity, leisure, more meaningful work, and culture. It doesn't buy love, but it does buy you a damn good shot at it. Money guarantees as best anything can that we'll get everything low on Maslow's hierarchy of needs, and thus enables us to work toward the values higher on the pyramid. Money even turns out to be the essential glue that binds people together, that enables and drives us to work together on a massive scale. What's not to love?

In the end, if you hate money—or are even indifferent to it—you must not understand what money does, or you have anti-human values. The hatred of money may not be the root of all evil, but it is a misguided hatred and a great evil indeed.

So far, I have argued that the love of money is reasonable, because money is a stand in and a means to a great number of goods worth wanting. Nevertheless, some people will balk. They complain that money or material wealth are evil because they in some way corrupt our character. Let's turn to their arguments more closely in the next chapter.

Three

> The immediate motive to productive activity in a market society is . . . typically some mixture of greed and fear . . . the motives of greed and fear are what the market brings to prominence, and that includes greed on behalf of, and fear for the safety of, one's family. Even when one's concerns are thus wider than those of one's mere self, the market posture is greedy and fearful in that one's opposite-number marketeers are predominantly seen as possible sources of enrichment, and as threats to one's success. These are horrible ways of seeing other people.
>
> —G. A. Cohen (2008)

In the previous chapter, I argued that the love of money is perfectly reasonable. Money makes mass cooperation possible. It buys us freedom, culture, literacy, safety, leisure, and peace. It insulates us from many threats and dangers, and so makes it easier to enjoy love and friendship.

But many readers might think that there's still something dirty about money. Their complaints might take either of these forms:

1. *Money and wealth corrupt us.* According to this objection, introducing money into human relationships makes people nastier, meaner, and more selfish.
2. *Money has an impure and profane meaning.* On this view, which I mentioned in Chapter 1, money has a social meaning. To

put a price on something is to communicate that the thing in question has no value as an end in itself, but instead is a mere commodity for consumption, something of merely instrumental value.

If these two complaints were true, then it would make sense to retain some residual distrust of money and material wealth. However, the complaints don't survive close scrutiny.

THE HAIFA DAY CARE STUDY

Proponents of the view that money corrupts love to cite a study from the 1970s. Supposedly, this study shows that introducing money into preexisting relationships can corrupt people, turning them more selfish and less concerned with how they affect others.

In the 1970s, some day care facilities in Haifa, Israel, had a problem with too many parents picking up their children late. At the time, parents faced no financial penalty for late pickups. Some economists then ran an experiment to see whether financial penalties would change parents' behavior.

You might expect that introducing a penalty would reduce the number of late pickups. The higher the penalty, the fewer late pickups there will be, and the less late parents will be. After all, that seems to follow from simple microeconomics. In general, the more expensive something is, the less of it people demand. If the "quantity-demanded" of late pickups is 10/day when the "price" of a late pickup is $0, then the quantity-demanded of late pickups when the price is $1/hour late should be much lower. Right?

That's not quite what the study found. At first, the economists introduced a small fine—less than $10 in today's money, adjusted for inflation. To their surprise, when this small penalty was introduced, the number of late pickups increased—in fact, it more than doubled.[1] When the penalty fee was then increased to a larger amount, an amount more painful to pay, the parents then started complying with the rules more and late pickups eventually dropped to near zero. It was no surprise that high fines stopped parents coming late. What was surprising was that going from no fines to small fines *increased* the number of late pickups.

Political theorist Michael Sandel and philosopher Debra Satz view this experiment as providing strong evidence that introducing money into relationships can have a corrupting effect on our character and concerns.[2] They interpret the experiment as showing that by introducing a small fine, the Israeli day care transformed the way parents thought of late pickups. Before the fines, they regarded late pickups as a moral transgression. Some picked their kids up late, sure, but they thought it was morally wrong. They felt bad for the workers they inconvenienced. But when a fine was introduced, according to Sandel and Satz, parents stopped seeing late pickups as a moral transgression. They cared less about the workers and felt less guilty. They instead regarded the late pickups as a just another financial transaction, in effect, a service provided for a price.

On this interpretation, introducing a small financial penalty actually reduced the overall cost that parents paid. When the fine was $0, parents still paid a cost in terms of emotional guilt. When the fine was small, they paid that small cash fine, but they no longer felt guilt. So the overall cost of late pickups was lower, and parents "quantity-demanded" of late pickups went up.

But there's a problem. The case is rather ambiguous. The reason it's ambiguous is because money means something. The price we attach to something means something too.

To explain, imagine that I constantly berate my students for turning in their weekly short papers late. They feel guilty about it, knowing that late papers mess up my schedule and make it harder to assign fair grades. Nevertheless, a few still turn in late papers. Finally, after a few weeks, I tell them enough is enough. Henceforth, if they pass in a paper late, I will penalize their grade on that paper . . . by 1 *percentage point*. You might expect the number of late papers to go up, not down.

The reason needn't be because introducing a penalty changes my students' attitudes, transforms our relationship, and stops them from caring about how they've inconvenienced me. Rather, it could be that the small penalty communicates information about the relative harm the late papers cause. Students would reasonably react by thinking, "Wow, I thought turning in papers late really put Prof. Brennan out. But now that he introduced a penalty of a mere point for a late paper, I realize I was mistaken to think that. That the penalty is so small means that it was never a big deal. I guess I shouldn't have ever felt guilty about it and I'll feel free to turn in papers late. My mistake."

The same issue applies to the Haifa case. Maybe the *small fine* inadvertently signaled to the parents that they had been mistaken to believe that picking up their kids really hurt the facility. If all it takes is a small fee to make the day care whole, then picking kids up late was never a big deal.

This experiment is too ambiguous. It doesn't show introducing money corrupts people. It may just show that a small fine communicates a small wrong.

DO MARKETS MAKE US NICE?

The Marxist philosopher G. A. Cohen frequently argued that market-based societies—that is, societies in which most economic activities and interactions between strangers are mediated by money and the concern for profit—would corrupt us. Markets induce people to cooperate with one another, but only out of some mixture of fear and greed. People are fearful of losing what they have and being subject to horrible deprivation. They are also greedy—they constantly want more for themselves. People cooperate with one another, not because they care about others or want to serve them for their own sake, but instead to get money for themselves. So, Cohen thought, having economies run on money would make it so that people just view each other as mere means for acquiring more money for themselves. They would stop caring about each other and become ever selfish.

One problem with Cohen's argument is that it's all done from the armchair. He does not provide any empirical evidence—nor does he cite any studies—showing that money or markets have these corrupting effects. Rather, he just consults his imagination. When he imagines his ideal society, he imagines a world free of money in which people cooperate with each other out of mutual concern and love. When he looks at actual commercial transactions, he just imagines that the real-life people engaging in such transactions have no fellow-feeling or mutual concern, but instead simply care about themselves. Since he was raised from birth to be a Marxist, he accepts his parents' claims that markets and money must corrupt us and make us even more selfish than we otherwise would be. But such imaginary exercises do not qualify as *evidence*.

Fortunately, there is a larger body of evidence in experimental economics examining effects of markets on people's behavior. This is our overall best evidence regarding how having human interactions mediated by money affects our behavior and out attitudes.

Economists have created a number of specially-designed games in which subjects can interact in various ways. Large sums of money—sometimes the equivalent of a month's pay—are at stake. In experimental economics games, to ensure the results are valid and do not simply reflect players' confusions, all subjects are taught the rules and are required to demonstrate an understanding of what is at stake. In general, the subjects who play these experiment games do not see or interact with each other outside of the game—they might even be on opposite sides of the world. This is important because it allows economists to control the incentives: subjects experience no external or extra incentive to play the games any particular way.

With that in mind, let's look at some examples of the games.

The Trust Game is designed to see whether players trust each other and whether they are worthy of the trust others place in them. The first player receives a fixed amount, such as $10. She is then given the option of sending some of her money to a second player. Every dollar she sends will be multiplied by three. Thus, if she gives the second player all $10, he'll in fact receive $30. The second player may then return as much as he wants back to the first player, or keep it all for himself. The questions tested: Will the first player trust the second player enough to send him some money, in hopes that he will split the increased pot? If the second player receives some money, will he reward the first player's trust or take advantage of her?

The Dictator Game is designed to see whether people will be unconditionally generous toward strangers when there is no hope of reward. Two subjects—who don't see each other or know each other—are selected. At random, one is selected to play the role of Dictator. He is given a lump sum of cash.

He may share as much as he pleases with the second player, or keep it all for himself. The question tested: Will the dictator share with the second player or be entirely selfish?

The Ultimatum Game is designed to see whether people will act out of a sense of fairness and whether they are willing to incur a personal cost to punish what they regard as unfair behavior. In this game, one player is assigned the role of Proposer; the other is made the Respondent. The Proposer is given a sum of money, say, $50. She must then propose a split of the cash with the Respondent. She may propose any split she wants, such as she gets $50 and the Respondent gets nothing, they split it $25 to $25, or anything else. The Respondent then either accepts the proposal or rejects it. If the Respondent accepts it, the money is split as proposed. If she rejects the split, they both get nothing. The questions tested: Will the Proposer— who has done nothing to earn the money—offer a fair amount?

There are other games testing other behaviors. Some test whether players will cooperate or cheat each other. Some test whether players will contribute to a common good or instead free ride on it. Some test whether players will preserve a common resource or overconsume it.

Various economists have played these games all around the world, sometimes for very large sums of money, looking to determine what factors induce or undermine trust, trustworthiness, cooperativeness, fairness, and so on. Contrary to what Cohen, Sandel, or other people suspicious of markets and money might think, the results are surprising.

Joseph Henrich and his colleagues summarize their work as follows:

> group-level differences in economic organization and the degree of market integration explain a substantial portion

of the behavioral variation across societies: *the higher the degree of market integration and the higher the payoffs to cooperation, the greater the level of cooperation in experimental games.*[3]

That is, selfishness abounds in non-market societies. In other words, in the societies where people most often and most routinely interact with strangers and in which cooperation is mediated by money in the pursuit of profit, people are fair, nice, generous, and cooperative; they tend to avoid free riding, they cheat less, and they are willing to incur a personal sacrifice to police unfair behavior. In general, people from market-based economies seem to have adopted a tendency to empathize with strangers and exhibit a stronger sense of fairness than people from non-market societies.

Economist Herbert Gintis explains:

> Movements for religious and lifestyle tolerance, gender equality, and democracy have flourished and triumphed in societies governed by market exchange, and nowhere else.
>
> My colleagues and I found dramatic evidence of this positive relationship between markets and morality in our study of fairness in simple societies—hunter-gatherers, horticulturalists, nomadic herders, and small-scale sedentary farmers—in Africa, Latin America, and Asia. Twelve professional anthropologists and economists visited these societies and played standard ultimatum, public goods, and trust games with the locals. As in advanced industrial societies, members of all of these societies exhibited a considerable degree of moral motivation and a willingness to sacrifice monetary gain to achieve fairness and reciprocity, even in anonymous one-shot situations. More interesting for our purposes, we measured the degree of

market exposure and cooperation in production for each society, and we found that the ones that regularly engage in market exchange with larger surrounding groups have more pronounced fairness motivations. The notion that the market economy makes people greedy, selfish, and amoral is simply fallacious.[4]

As it turns out, empirically, the strongest cultural predictor that participants will play fairly with strangers is how market-oriented their society is. Indeed, there is strong evidence that in general, market societies are the most tolerant and have the least corruption in their political institutions.[5]

Let's look at some other studies. You might think of a competitive market as dog-eat-dog and cutthroat. However, in one major study, economists Patrick Francois and Tanguy van Ypersele discovered that the more competitive a market is, the more trust, rather than less, people have toward one another.[6] To non-economists, this may seem surprising. To economists, less so. The more competitive a market is, the less any individual can push others around or exert undue influence on each other. They are made to play fair.

Recently, Dan Ariely and his colleagues have studied the residual effects of communism and capitalism on people's cheating behavior. They recruited a number of German citizens of similar socioeconomic backgrounds, all of whom lived in Berlin. Some had families from the former socialist East Germany, others from the capitalist West Germany. They found that people who used to live in or who were raised by parents from East Germany lie and cheat at a significantly higher rate than those from West Germany.[7]

Relatedly, psychologist Paul Zak and economist Stephen Knack have found that market-oriented societies also tend to be high-trust societies, while non-market societies tend to be low-trust societies.[8] One of the major questions about any society is whether its inhabitants exhibit what economists call **generalized social trust**. Generalized social trust refers to when people expect that strangers—including waiters, auto mechanics, lawyers, or others with whom they do business—will do their part, keep their word, fulfill their contracts on time, be honest in their representations, avoid stealing or taking advantage of others, and so on. It turns out that different societies have different levels of generalized social trust. New Zealand has far higher levels of generalized social trust than, say, Venezuela or Russia. While many cultural, historical, demographic, and institutional factors influence generalized social trust, it turns out that there is a very strong positive correlation between how market-oriented an economy is and the level of generalized social trust. This appears to be a causal relationship rather than a mere correlation. As countries become more economically liberal, they tend to also then develop higher levels of trust. Again, in the societies where people's interactions with strangers are most mediated by money and motivated by the pursuit of profit, in fact such strangers trust each other and have high regard for each other's morals.

Philosophers tend to assume that money has a kind of profane, utilitarian meaning. Thinking in terms of money, they presume, will induce us to act in selfish ways. On the contrary, economists Omar Al-Ubaydli, Daniel Houser, and colleagues have shown that "priming" people with words related to markets, money, and trade makes them *more* (not less!) trusting, trustworthy, and fair in experiments.[9] Many philosophers have argued, on the contrary, that introducing a market mindset, or reminding people about the concepts of money and profit, would somehow cause them to switch modes of thinking, moving from pro-social attitudes toward more selfish behaviors. On the contrary, Al-Ubaydli and his colleagues have run a wide range of experimental economics games in which people have the opportunities to exhibit various moral dispositions. They find that experimental groups who are made to think about market-oriented concepts behave *better* and in a more pro-social way than control groups who are not so primed. That is, when we get people into the market mindset, they become *nicer*.

Economists Mitchell Hoffman and John Morgan found, contrary to everyone's expectations, that "adult populations deliberately selected from two cutthroat internet industries—domain trading and adult entertainment (pornography)" are "more pro-social than [undergraduate] students: they are more altruistic, trusting, trustworthy, and lying averse."[10] Many economists and philosophers assume that only the most cutthroat and nasty people will choose to work in such industries, but in fact, the actual actors play nicer than others.

One recent study by Gabriele Camera and his colleagues found more ambiguous results than that. The BBC reported that the study discovered that "money can reduce trust in groups."[11] But that's a misleading summary of the study. Camera and his colleagues played a series of experimental games in which people could choose to cooperate or not, and could choose to be generous or selfish when cooperating.[12] They found that introducing money into small groups made players more selfish and less cooperative—as the BBC reported. But they *also* found that introducing money into large groups made them less selfish and more cooperative.

Perhaps the negative half of this experiment is not so surprising—in Western cultures, money is seen as impersonal. So introducing money into small-scale, personal interactions signals estrangement. If you introduce money into a small-scale relationship, you signal an intention to have a more instrumental relationship. Yet, in large-scale communities and among strangers, introducing money enables trust. It's a sign of cooperativeness and a willingness to play fair.

Back in the 1970s, sociologist Richard Titmuss claimed that introducing money and financial incentives into certain spheres of life would have a massive corrupting effect. He claimed that paying for blood donations would result in there being fewer overall willing donors and would also reduce the quality of the donated blood. The reason, he claimed, would be that offering money for donations would induce us to replace our altruistic motives—the desire to help those in need—with selfish financial ones. He claimed that under such conditions that unless the price of blood were very high, few people would donate. Further, he claimed that financial incentives would lead only the least healthy people—alcoholics, the homeless, the desperately poor—to sell blood and so lead to lower quality blood supplies on average.

Titmuss's studies did not follow proper scientific procedures; he used data from uncontrolled experiments and non-scientific surveys. Recently, researchers Nicola Lacetera, Mario Macis, and Robert Slonim have done a series of proper scientific experiments to see how money or other incentives affect blood donations. They found, contrary to Titmuss, that economic incentives such as gift cards do in fact increase blood donations and do not affect the quality of the blood received.[13]

More recently, William English and Peter Jaworski gained access to a massive data set on nearly every paid plasma clinic in the United States. The data showed not merely where the clinics are located, but how much paid blood was collected in any given month over a period of more than a decade. Using this data, they were able to prove not merely that paid plasma leads to an overall higher supply of blood. They were also able to show that for most plasma sellers, altruistic concerns remain a significant reason why they supply blood. They found that, pace Titmuss, the blood came from higher, not lower, quality "sources." But most intriguing of all, they found that when a paid plasma clinic enters an area and advertises for paid plasma, in both the short and long term, this induces more people to donate blood for free at the Red Cross and elsewhere. Paid plasma not only increases the supply of blood overall, but actually increases the supply of donated blood.[14]

In fact, these results seem to generalize. Psychologist Judy Cameron recently analyzed 96 distinct experimental studies that compared subjects who received an extrinsic reward to those who received no reward.[15] She found that in general, rewarding people for performing a task does not remove their intrinsic motivation for doing it; it may add an additional selfish motivation, but it does not remove or substitute for other motivations.

THE SUPPOSED MEANING OF MONEY

The empirical evidence generally shows that introducing money into our relationships does not crowd out or reduce noble or altruistic motives. On the contrary, people in the most money-mediated societies tend to exhibit more virtue than others. Why, then, do so many people assume money and material goods will corrupt us?

One reason, I suspect, has to do with the peculiar meaning Westerners impose on money. As I mentioned in Chapter One, Westerner's view money as "ordinary, mundane, impersonal, and neutral. It is profane, with only quantitative meanings."[16]

Money "signifies a sphere of 'economic' relationships which are inherently impersonal, transitory, amoral and calculating."[17]

It's worth noting that this view of money is not universal. In American culture today, giving a cash gift for a birthday may seem "thoughtless." To be "thoughtful," you're supposed to anticipate the kinds of things your loved one enjoys in order to signal you understand their preferences.

Sociologist Viviana Zelizer's extensive work on the meaning of money and exchange, work spread out over multiple books, seems to show us that the supposed "profanity" of money is not a universal idea, but rather a peculiarity of our own culture at this particular time. In her work, Zelizer uncovers many other instances where different cultures at different times did not impute the meaning to money or to markets that Sandel and other critics of money thinks we should impute.[18]

Sociologists Maurice Bloch and Jonathan Parry concur:

The problem seems to be that for us money signifies a sphere of "economic" relationships which are inherently impersonal, transitory, amoral and calculating. There is therefore something profoundly awkward about offering it as a gift expressive of relationships which are supposed to be personal, enduring, moral and altruistic. But clearly this awkwardness derives from the fact that here money's "natural" environment—the "economy"—is held to constitute an autonomous domain to which general moral precepts do not apply. . . . Where it is not seen as a separate and amoral domain, where the economy is 'embedded' in society and subject to its moral laws, monetary relations are rather unlikely to be represented as the antithesis of bonds of kinship and friendship, and there is consequently nothing inappropriate about making gifts of money to cement such bonds.[19]

Like Zelizer, Bloch and Parry conclude that money and markets do not have the same meaning everywhere that they have here. Instead, the reason commodification seems so repugnant to us Westerners is because we Westerners tend to regard the sphere of exchange and money as a "separate and amoral domain." Bloch, Parry, and Zelizer say that we then mistakenly assume that this is just a "natural" or essential fact about money. In fact, it's just a meaning Westerners impute to money.

For instance, in some cultures, such as the Merina people of Madagascar, it's normal for a husband to pay his wife after sex. Rather than this signaling patriarchy or signaling that sex is a mere service the husband buys from his wife, it's actually a way of signaling respect for her reproductive power. It's less like buying coffee and more like saying a prayer. This works for the Merina because they don't attach the same nasty meaning to money that, well, you the reader might. It seems icky and weird to you not because it's icky and weird, but because you think money is icky. It's a meaning you impose on their interaction, a meaning they don't share.

Bloch and Parry claim we can generally find real-life examples where people of different cultures buy and sell something Westerners find repugnant to buy and sell, but for the people in those cultures, buying and selling has a very different meaning than what it has for us Westerners.[20] We Westerners could attach different meanings to markets than we do.

Similarly, it's not seen as impersonal in some cultures to give gifts of money. Jewish people do during Bar and Bat Mitzvahs or Chinese people do during New Year's. That was once even true in the West. In the US in the late 1800s, giving a cash gift was seen as especially thoughtful, rather than less thoughtful, as it is now. (Perhaps richer societies see money as less thoughtful because money is so easy to acquire. Taking the time to learn someone else's preferences becomes a stronger signal of concern when time becomes scarcer than money.)

In *Pricing the Priceless Child*, Zelizer claims that the development of life insurance and tort law largely explains why people in the West today view their children as having a kind of sacred value. In the late 19th century, children started working less (on the farm or in factories). They thus stopped being economic assets to their parents and started being net economic burdens. How, then, would courts price the life of a child—an economic burden—in a wrongful death tort? How should life insurance deal with their deaths?

As Zelizer documents at length, what happened was that, in deciding to put a price on children's lives, people started to think of children as "priceless," as possessing a special kind of value not shared even by adults. The current attitudes we have towards children—seeing them as in some way sacred—developed *as a result* of trying to price children once we stopped seeing them as an economic asset.[21] So, contrary to what one might expect, putting a monetary price on things is sometimes the very thing that makes us come to see those things as "priceless."

My point here is that one reason why people expect money and material goods to be corrupting is that they have accepted, uncritically, a certain view of the meaning of money common to Westerners today. But this meaning is a social construct. It's a fiction Westerners impose on money, not a meaning built into money itself. Not everyone shares this meaning. (I don't.) You don't have to either—you are free to reject it. But at the very least, you should stop assuming money will corrupt us because it's inherently icky. Again, the ickiness is something in your head, not something in the money.

THE PRICE OF EVERYTHING AND
THE VALUE OF EVERYTHING

The empirical evidence not only fails to show that money has a corrupting effect, but generally shows that money has an ameliorative effect on our character. Nevertheless, many philosophers and laypeople might respond by saying that this is all beside the point. Instead, some think that the desire to make a profit is itself an inherently corrupt desire. I'll respond to that view in the next chapter. Still others think that attaching monetary prices to things—as markets are apt to do—is inherently incompatible with thinking of things as having intrinsic value. Philosophers and political theorists such Elizabeth Anderson, Margaret Jane Radin, Benjamin Barber, and Michael Sandel, among others, claim that to put a price on something is to signify or express that the thing in question only has instrumental value, that its value consists in its ability to satisfy our desires, and/or that it must be fungible without loss with anything else of the same price.

After all, they say, isn't that what it means to put a price on something? If you say a pack of gum is worth $1, aren't you thereby saying that the value it has is equivalent to the value of a one-dollar bill? But a dollar bill has no value in itself. It's just an instrument for getting other things and for satisfying our desires. Thus, the argument goes, to say a pack of gum is worth $1 is to say that it is fungible and has merely instrumental value.

That seems fine, they say, for a pack of gum. But some things, they claim, have a value that can't be expressed in terms of a monetary price. For instance, many people think that human lives have a kind of sacred value, a value money lacks. Humans beings are ends-in-themselves, while money is not. Thus, they worry, if we attach a price to human life, we're somehow denigrating it or failing to respect life's real value.

For instance, when the US government considers whether to impose certain safety regulations or accept certain risks, it tries to compare the monetary costs of such regulations to the value of saving a human life. It generally assigns a value of $7.5 million to one life. Some philosophers balk at this, saying that you can't assign any such price. After all, if the US government says a human life is worth $7.5 million, isn't the government thereby expressing that human life has the same kind of value money does? Worse, isn't it saying that one human life has the same kind of value as 7.5 million packs of gum?

The answer to both questions is no. In fact, these objections rest on a serious misunderstanding of the meaning of prices and of utility theory in economics. To explain why, I'll have to get a bit technical.

Consider a person, whom I'll call Rational Randy. Randy is a perfectly rational economic actor. (Real-life people may not be, but Randy is.) Randy has what economists call a utility function, which means that in light of his preferences and values, we can rank all possible states of affairs from best to worst. Ties are permitted. If Randy is indifferent between A and B, then A and B occupy the same spot on his utility function.

So far, all of this is compatible with thinking that some things have intrinsic value. I think my spouse and my dog have intrinsic value, but I would choose to save my spouse over my dog. I think *Guernica* and the last Father's Day card my kids gave me have intrinsic value and are ends-in-themselves, but I would choose to save the former over the latter.

Note that to say that Randy has a utility function is not to say that Randy thinks all values reduce to one common denominator called "utility." It's not to say that all things have only one kind of value, a value called utility. Randy can recognize that there is a plurality of different kinds of values. "Utility" in the economist's sense isn't the fundamental value all things have. Rather, utility is just the way economists represent Randy's preference rankings, in light of his values.

If you want, imagine that Randy has all the correct moral preferences, whatever those are. This is still compatible with him having a utility function. If, from a moral point of view, A is superior to or preferable to B, that's what Randy will choose. If from a moral point of view, there is no way to choose between A and B, then Randy will be indifferent between them and they'll occupy the same spot on his utility curve.

Most critics of prices and money are fine with everything I've said so far. They accept that Randy can have what's called an ordinal utility function, that is, a simple ranking of all states of affairs from better to worse. After all, part of what philosophers' moral theories are supposed to do is tell us how to rank and evaluate things as better or worse, from a moral point of view.

But economists don't stop there. They think Randy not only has an ordinal utility function, but also a cardinal utility function. An ordinal utility function simply ranks things: best, second best, third best. But a cardinal utility function goes further: It puts an exact number on each choice on some common scale. A cardinal utility function can say that A has a value of 10.37534983, B a value of 8.4343999, C a value of 2.4, and so on. Many moral theorists (such as those I mentioned earlier) worry that putting things on cardinal utility function with prices somehow is incompatible with things having intrinsic value.

Isn't saying that everything has value equal *overall* to some monetary price just saying that everything's value *just is* its monetary price? Isn't putting everything on this precise scale thus saying that everything has only one kind of value, utility?

Again, the answer is no. In the 1940s, Jonathan von Neumann and Oskar Morgenstern produced a mathematical proof to the contrary. They showed that if you accept a few basic axioms about how rational people respond to *lotteries* and deal with *risk* (e.g., that rational people prefer better prizes to worse prizes and prefer better odds to worse odds), then one can mathematically translate any ordinal utility function into a cardinal utility function. That is, given A) Randy's ranking of all possible states of the world and B) Randy's rational way of choosing among lotteries, we generate C) a new utility function, in which all values can be expressed on a cardinal, numerical scale.[22] If we suppose that Randy also values money, we'll then be able to express this scale in monetary terms. It turns out that *every* possible set of trade-offs a rational agent might have, regardless of whether that agent is selfish or altruistic, amoral, immoral, or moral, a value monist or a pluralist, a Kantian or a utilitarian, can be expressed in monetary terms on a continuous, numerical utility scale.

Again, that's not to say that the only thing that the agent really values is utility, money, or self-satisfaction, but just to say that we can correctly represent the agent's values on this one scale. All of this is compatible with holding something to have more than instrumental value, or that not everything is fungible with money, or that there is a plurality of values. Economists can and do accept all that.

I realize this is all very abstract. I'm responding to an abstract complaint that philosophers make by pointing out their complaint is based on a misunderstanding—or at least obsolete understanding—of economic theory.

Let's take another stab at it, this time less abstract. Philosophers claim that there are at least two different kinds of value things can have. To say something is intrinsically valuable is to say it is valuable as an end in itself, that it is valuable for its own sake. For instance, happiness is an end in itself. To say something is instrumentally valuable is to say it is valued as a means to getting something else. Money is instrumentally valuable but not an end in itself. (Some things have both kinds of value. A Starbucks barista is both an end in herself and useful as a means to getting good coffee.)

Philosophers often complain that to put a price on something somehow lowers the kind of value the thing has. They say some things have intrinsic value, but to put a price on it is to say it's equivalent to something of merely instrumental value.

Economists disagree; they say this misunderstands what money does and what it means to represent choices in terms of monetary prices. Instead, money is a way of representing the trade-offs we have to make. It's a way of making explicit what you have to give up when you choose one thing over another. That's all.

Putting a price on something doesn't tell us how someone values the thing in question. I regard $100,000 as being of mere instrumental value, and worth $100,000. I regard a 15th wedding anniversary trip with my wife as being of some intrinsic value, not merely instrumental value. But I wouldn't pay $100,000 for that trip, not because I don't love my wife or can't be bothered to celebrate my marriage, but because of everything else I'd have to give up to take that trip for that price.

The good thing about money prices is that they make explicit what we lose when we choose one thing over another.

If you have $10,000 to spend on either A) life-saving surgery for your son, B) life-saving surgery for your dog, or C) a sick new surfboard, you'd probably choose A over B or C. Indeed, you'd probably be willing to pay a lot more for A than B or C. That's not because you value your son the same way you value money, but precisely because you see your son's life as having a different and higher kind of value than money.

CONCLUSION

Some people think it's not OK to love money because they regard money as dirty, profane, and corrupting. But, as we saw, that's not what the evidence shows. Money facilitates cooperation among strangers. Societies in which relationships are frequently mediated by money are also more open, trusting, and honest societies. Insofar as money seems dirty, the dirtiness is something some Westerners project onto money, not something inherent in the money itself.

Four

> [B]ehind all this pain, death and destruction there is the stench of what Basil of Caesarea called "the dung of the devil." An unfettered pursuit of money rules. The service of the common good is left behind. Once capital becomes an idol and guides people's decisions, once greed for money presides over the entire socioeconomic system, it ruins society, it condemns and enslaves men and women, it destroys human fraternity, it sets people against one another and, as we clearly see, it even puts at risk our common home.[1]
>
> —Pope Francis, 2015

Sometimes we disagree about which things are good or bad not because we have different moral standards, but because we disagree about the relevant facts.

For instance, both anti-vaxxers and medical doctors think it's good to save lives. They both think health matters. They both hate watching babies die. It's not as though the anti-vaxxers say, "Sure, vaccines save lives and rarely have serious side effects, but I oppose them because I love to watch babies die." Anti-vaxxers advocate policies which kill babies, but they don't mean to.

The difference between pro- and anti-vaccine crowds isn't over *moral values*; it's over how vaccines work. And, in this case, the anti-vaxxers oppose vaccines because they are misinformed about how vaccines work and what the relevant risks are.

All this applies to common people's views of markets, profit, and money. As we saw in Chapters One and Three, many people in the West think money has a dirty meaning. They think profit is evil—to make a profit is just to harm others. They think rich people are bad people. They believe wanting money is base and degenerate.

These are not basic moral beliefs. Rather, these beliefs depend in part on empirical views about what money does to us, what profit is, what it takes to make a profit, and how markets work. People's *moral assessment* of money, profit, and business depend upon their beliefs about *economics*. So, sure, Karl Marx and Pope Francis hate business and market economies, but they also accept discredited, unscientific economic theories. They are the anti-vaxxers of economics.

We can't make an intelligent moral evaluation of money, markets, profits, or the rich until we get the facts right. We need to know how the economy works. We need to know what profit is and where it comes from. We need to know how people make their money. We need to know how trade works. We also need to know what happens when we invest it or when we give it all away.

People denigrate money-making because they don't understand it. So, step one in defending the desires to have money, to make money, and to keep it, is to explain how market economies work.

MORAL HARDWARE FOR A LONG DEAD WORLD

One of my business school colleagues asks his MBA students, "From whom did you learn morality?" They give sensible answers: their parents, pastors, friends, teachers, and neighbors.

He then asks, "Why, then, did serial killer John Wayne Gacy or Unabomber Ted Kaczynski kill all those people? Did their parents forget to teach them right from wrong?" The students pause. He says, "No, there's something messed up about their brains."

He explains that the extant psychological and anthropological research shows that we've evolved to be moral, social animals.[2] Our ancestors over the past hundred thousand generations lived mostly in family-based clans or tribes of around 100 or so people. They depended heavily on in-group cooperation—and, it turns out, on a tendency to distrust people outside that narrow group. For these groups to succeed, people needed to be disposed to work together for the common good and to be willing to punish people who tried to free ride on others' work. We're descended from the cooperators, not the defectors. We have a kind of basic morality—a sense of right and wrong, a sense of fair and unfair—hardwired into our brains. Our parents and pastors are mostly teaching us about how to apply our basic moral intuitions rather than implanting those intuitions in the first place.

There's psychological evidence that even small babies have built-in moral dispositions and attitudes.[3] At three months old, babies can distinguish fair from unfair, kind from mean, helpful from hindering, and prefer the fair, kind, and helpful people. (They also have a preference for the familiar and known, and exhibit bigotry toward the different. Remember that our ancestors evolved to distrust outsiders.) As we get older, we further develop and better learn to act upon our moral emotions. But the hardware is largely there at birth.

The problem we face is that this built-in moral hardware was developed for a different world than the one we now live in. As moral psychologist Paul Bloom explains:

Our emotions have evolved for simpler times. They are not well calibrated for the modern world, where we are surrounded by countless strangers and have access to cars, guns, and the Internet.

All of the moral emotions can have disastrous effects. . . . I think this is true even for empathy—the capacity to put yourself in someone else's shoes, to feel their pleasure and their pain. When it comes to personal relationships, empathy can be a good thing—I wouldn't want a parent, a child, or a spouse who lacked empathy. But, just as with anger, empathy doesn't scale. It is because of our empathetic responses that we care more about a little girl stuck in a well than about billions being affected in the future by climate change. The girl elicits empathy; statistical future harms do not. To the extent that we can recognize, and act upon, serious threats that don't have identifiable victims, we are relying on rational deliberation, not gut responses.[4]

Stalin is rumored to have said the death of one person is a tragedy, while the death of millions is a statistic. The quotation is probably apocryphal, but whoever said it was right. The first 9500 or so generations of homo sapiens were making moral decisions that affected at most a hundred people. They didn't have to—and so did not—think in terms of millions or billions.

We evolved to live in small, hunter-gatherer groups of closely related individuals, with infrequent and often belligerent contact with outsiders. Our ancestors had a primitive subsistence-level hunter-gatherer economy. They traded sometimes with other human groups, but most of their production was internal to the group. Internally, they relied more on favors, direct giving with the expectation of reciprocity, and on family-style giving than they did on money, contracts, and trade. Their notions of property were undeveloped because they had little and most of what they had they consumed immediately.

That's the kind of economy they had—and that's the kind of cooperation our moral architecture evolved to help facilitate. Your moral intuitions are designed to help you be a successful cooperator in hunter-gatherer group of 100 people or less.

But that's not how we now live. Everything in your home or office was built collectively, by millions of strangers who didn't even know they were working together or that they were helping build all that stuff. Every day, you probably interact and cooperate with dozens of strangers, most of whom you'll never see again. You need to be able to plan not only for tomorrow's meals but for situations (such as paying for college or retirement) decades in the future.

Our ancestors needed—and evolved to have—the kinds of moral norms that help facilitate cooperation in face-to-face interaction among familiar people in small groups. Today, we instead need the moral norms that facilitate impersonal cooperation among strangers on the scale of billions. Our moral architecture, our moral intuitions, our built-in moral emotions are designed for the kinds of lives our ancestors lived, not the lives we now lead. Our moral brains are built for the stone-age tribal life on the African savannah, not modern life in New York City.

The upshot of this is that perhaps we shouldn't be surprised that people have so much built-in suspicion of money, markets, extended trade, trade with strangers across borders, corporations, the profit/loss mechanism, contracts, stocks, bonds, debt, option markets, and so on. The institution, rules, and norms that make extended cooperation possible don't follow or mimic the rules that make tribal cooperation work. These things are all too new and our built-in moral architecture hasn't caught up. For the primitive moral modules in our brains, new things like money and markets are scary and weird.

MORAL SOFTWARE FOR A RECENTLY DECEASED WORLD

We're born with moral ideas, but our cultures teach us to apply these ideas in new and interesting ways. That's partly why certain moral ideas—e.g., don't eat babies for fun, don't marry your brother—are universal, but others—e.g., tolerate religious differences, accept homosexuality, respect freedom of the press—are not.

Sure, we have "cave man" moral brains, but we also inherit various cultural norms. We've had a few thousand years' worth of experience living in "civilization." So, shouldn't our moral ideas have caught up with the way we live and work?

Well, perhaps not. The problem is that throughout most of human history, there has been something like a fixed stock of wealth. There was almost no growth in total income or wealth. As the economist John Maynard Keynes puts it:

> From the earliest times of which we have record . . . down to the beginning of the eighteenth century, there was no very great change in the standard of life of the average man. . . . Ups and downs certainly. Visitations of plague, famine, and war. Golden intervals. But no progressive, violent change. Some periods perhaps 50 per cent better than others—at the utmost 100 per cent better than before—in the four thousand years which ended (say) in A.D. 1700.[5]

Many exciting political and cultural changes occurred over those thousands of years. The birth and death of empires. Great wars. Religions rising and falling. Great discoveries, great forgettings, and great rediscoveries in science. But from an economic point of view, pretty much nothing happened. Everyone everywhere except for a few kings, lords, and high priests was desperately poor, with no hope of getting richer. If there was a good harvest, people would have a few more babies, but the extra population would eat up all the extra production, and most everyone would remain the same. From early civilization onward, economic history consists of thousands of years of the typical person being an illiterate, malnourished peasant.

Further, throughout most of history, most of the rich people—the kings, the nobles, and the high priests—got rich by stealing from the poor. Or, more charitably, they got rich by offering protection and salvation in exchange for taxes and tithes. They used this money to wage expensive wars and build lavish palaces while the peasants starved. The kings and high priests took a share of rice from each of their subjects, subjects who had little rice to spare, but didn't do much to make their subjects better off in return beyond, at best, preventing various invasions. It's plausible to think that for most of history, most rich people were mostly parasites.

How does all this bear on our moral judgments? In light of economic conditions, for most of human history in most places, it was reasonable for everyone to believe this:

> There is a fixed amount of pie to go around. When the rich get a bigger slice of pie, there is automatically less pie for me. Indeed, all the rich people got rich by taking pie from the rest of us. Every bite the rich enjoy comes at our expense.

Jesus said it was hard for a rich man to get into heaven. One reason that might make sense was that for most of human history, the rich got rich by making other people *worse off*. It was reasonable to be suspicious of rich people.

But economic systems changed. Starting around the 1500s or so in Europe, and later elsewhere, market-oriented, bourgeois, commercial societies displaced the old feudal, imperial, and theocratic societies. Instead of simply changing who gets the big and small slices of pie, the new systems *made more pie*. Lots of it. Remember, as we discussed in Chapter One, the *typical* person today in England is at least 30 times richer than her counterpart 1000 years ago. The US today, by itself, produces in real terms 80–100 times more "pie" than the entire world did 1000 years ago. A typical person in Singapore is about 23 times richer than her counterpart was in 1960. When capitalism replaced feudalism, the capitalists grew rich, sure. But do did everyone else. That had never happened before, and it has only happened in market-oriented societies.

The new market systems didn't just make more pie. They didn't just do a better job ensuring that the "poor" got lots of pie. They also fundamentally changed the logic—the rules— about how you get rich.

In medieval England, the best way to get rich was to receive land from the king. Your peasants, who were not free to leave that land or to learn a trade, worked to put bread on your table. Sure, you protected them from . . . the other lords, I suppose. But you weren't doing much to improve their lives.

But commercial, bourgeois society changed the rules. In those societies, the most effective way to get rich is to make other people better off. Indeed, the more people you make better off, and the better off you make them, the richer you get. Let's take a look.

The average person relies upon a naïve heuristic, a heuristic which probably served our tribal ancestors well: There are two types of motives, altruistic and selfish. When people act on altruistic motives, they help others. When people act on selfish motives, they hurt others. Simple.

As we saw in Chapter One, people today extend this heuristic to evaluate organizations: They assume that a non-profit organization by definition helps people, while a for-profit organization by definition preys upon them.

There are many problems with this heuristic. One of the big problems is that motives and outcomes often come apart. Someone can mean well but do harm, while someone can be selfish but do a lot of good.

Imagine Betty Benevolence only wants to help others, but she has false beliefs about how to do so. When she sees someone on fire, she mistakenly believes the best way to help them is to drench them in gasoline. Betty intends to help, but she in fact makes things worse. In contrast, imagine Sammy Selfishness cares only about getting status, money, and fame for himself. He realizes the best way to promote his own ends is to cure cancer, so he does. Sammy Selfishness may only care about himself, but he does far more good for others than Betty or most people do.

A similar point holds for not-for-profit and for-profit organizations. Plenty of not-for-profit nongovernmental organizations (NGOs), government agencies, and charities do more harm than good. They waste resources. Some even are counterproductive, like Betty. They intend to help but in fact make things worse.[6]

More importantly, as we'll discuss here, many for-profit organizations make people better off—indeed, the general rule in a proper market is that the more profit you make, the more value you provide for others.

Most people have a bifurcated theory of human nature. They think businesspeople are motivated by greed, while government agents, soldiers, church leaders, NGO employees, and college professors are motivated by love and kindness. Not quite.

There are for-profit and not-for-profit *enterprises*. But there are no not-for-profit *people*. Rather, most people are selfish most of the time. Most people have a limited budget of altruistic concern for strangers. Doctors, nurses, public school teachers, college professors, government employees, and so on, are not volunteers. They do their jobs for money, so they can buy nice houses, vacations, gadgets, and whatever they need for their hobbies. They are—just like businesspeople—motivated to gain status, power, and influence for themselves. They are not sociopaths or devils, but neither are they angels. Rather, regardless of whether people work for government, NGOs, or business, people are people.

The real issue isn't whether people are altruistically or selfishly motivated—most people are mostly selfish most of the time, and altruistic only some of the time. Rather, the real issue is whether in their pursuit of personal profit, they make others better off or worse off. Does the pursuit of private self-interest produce a public benefit or a public harm? Does the pursuit of private self-interest hurt others or help them?

AS IF BY AN INVISIBLE HAND

The answer to those questions: It depends. It depends not only on local circumstance, but on the background rules.

Adam Smith—the founder of modern economics— understood this well. When you live in a feudal system where the only way to make a profit is to murder your neighbors and take their land, that's what people will do. If you live in a communist/socialist state where the best way to make a profit is to capture government agencies and exploit the citizens, that's what you'll do. If you live in a market society characterized by free trade, where the best way you make a profit is by providing a good or service that others value more highly than money they'd have to pay you to provide it, then you'll do that. The same self-interested profit-motive that induces us to prey upon each other in feudal or communist societies induces us in market society—as if guided by an invisible hand—to serve one another instead.

Let me describe a game I play in an economics and philosophy course I teach each semester. I bring in 45 distinct candy bars. I randomly assign each student a piece of candy. I ask them each to rate the candy they received on a scale from 1–10, with 1 meaning "I can't imagine a more disgusting individual piece of candy" and 10 meaning "This is the best candy bar I know of." I write their scores on the board.

Then I say, "You have 15 minutes to trade candy with each other. Feel free to make as many trades as you can." When the 15 minutes is up, I ask them to rate the candy they now have.

Inevitably, the scores shift upward. People who started at a 1 or 2 usually end up at a 6, 7, or 8. On average, even in my small classes, the total scores go up by about 50%. No one is made worse off, and almost everyone is made better off.

The game illustrates what economists call gains from trade. The logic of gains from trade is simple. Ana has a Snickers and Blake has M&Ms. They each have the right to say no—to unilaterally veto a trade. A trade takes place only if they both agree to it. If they're motivated by profit, they'll trade with each other only if Ana values Blake's M&Ms more than her Snickers, and Blake also values Ana's Snickers more than his M&Ms. In other words, a trade takes place only if both participants benefit from—profit from—the trade.

Trade is a paradigmatic example of a mutually beneficial interaction—or what economists call a "positive-sum game." A positive-sum game is a situation where the rules tend to ensure that all the players win.

Most games, such as poker or basketball, are what economists call "zero-sum." In zero-sum games, winning comes at someone else's expense. Winning money in poker requires that other people *lose* money. In poker games, money gets moved around, but no money gets made. If players start with $500 total among five players, they'll leave with $500 total.

But positive-sum games are different. In a positive-sum game, when you win, that doesn't make other people lose. Imagine a new game called "magic poker." In magic poker, every time someone wins a hand, not only do you acquire extra money, but the other players acquire more money too. In magic poker, when you win cash, the other players also win cash. In magic poker, if the players bring $500 total to the table, they walk away with $1000 total. If each player starts with $100, she leaves the table with no less than $100, and usually with more than $100. In magic poker, money doesn't just get moved around, but gets made.

Trade is like magic poker, not regular poker. Regular poker is zero-sum, while magic poker is positive-sum.

The great thing about trade is that it remains positive-sum even if the participants have few options, and even if their options are so bad that we wouldn't want to call the participants "fully autonomous."

Imagine, for instance, that before we play the trading game, one of my students had to skip breakfast and lunch, and so has terrible hunger pangs. Imagine she starts with a Mounds bar, but she hates coconut. She is desperate to get a Snickers bar, since Snickers really satisfies. Even under these bad conditions, she won't end up *worse* off during the trading game. At worst, she ends up with the Mounds she started with. Most likely, she will trade it for something she considers better than a Mounds. Suppose she ends up with a Hershey's Special Dark bar. Though that's not her favorite bar, the fact that she ends up with it tells us something important: This was her best available option, and she is better off than when she started. The lesson: Trade *increases* people's options, even when everyone acts selfishly.

During the Candy Game, most students only look out for themselves. Sometimes students will donate candy to others who really want it, but that happens only once every few years. Nevertheless, the rules of the Candy Game ensure that when students pursue their self-interest, they help other people too.

Back to Adam Smith: The pursuit of self-interest—or of profit—is neither inherently good nor inherently bad. Whether it is good or bad depends upon the background rules of interaction. The basic rules of trade are 1) a trade takes place only if both parties agree and 2) you cannot coerce the other party into agreeing. These rules are sufficient to ensure that to make a profit for yourself, you have to make a profit for others.[7] This means a company can profit from its suppliers only if the suppliers profit from selling to the company. A company can profit from its employees only if the employees profit from working for the company. A company can profit from its customers only if the customers profit from buying from the company. All this holds even if the some of the participants only have bad options.

MARKET COMPETITION IS COMPETITION
TO COOPERATE

Economists extol the virtues of competitive markets. As you'll soon see, they are right to do so. But the term "competitive" makes markets seem kind of nasty and bad. This is one reason why the Marxist philosopher G. A. Cohen asserted that markets are an inherently repugnant way for us to relate to one another.[8] He regarded markets as systems built on fear, greed, and selfishness. He thought socialist societies—in imagination if not in practice—illustrate how to live together on feelings of love, mutual concern, and reciprocity.

For most people, talk of competition connotes that markets are a kind of race. But that's misleading in at least three ways. Races are zero-sum games, where the winner wins at the expense of the losers. As we just saw, markets are positive-sum game. To win means to make a trade that benefits you, but you can do so only if you also benefit your trading partners. It's also misleading because in market systems, we do far more cooperating than we do competing.

One thing people miss about market competition is *competition to cooperate*. The landscaping companies that advertise in my neighborhood are competing against each other, sure. Yet what they compete for is the opportunity to cooperate—to make mutually beneficial, reciprocal trades with people in my neighborhood. It's a contest to decide who gets to serve others.

To a layperson, if you hear that a market is "highly competitive," you imagine a kind of winner-take-all, losers-get-nothing situation. A perfectly competitive market sounds scarier than a less competitive market. But that's a mistake. Rather, the more competitive the market is, the less power any individual has to push other people around. The more competitive a market is, the more gains from trade people realize, and the more the market price reflects the knowledge and values of all the people involved.

Competition prevents us from taking advantage of one another. Indeed, it's the most effective way to ensure that even the poor and desperate cannot be exploited. To illustrate, let's take a modified example from the classical economist David Ricardo.[9]

Imagine Starvin' Marvin wanders into a new town, desperate for work. If he doesn't eat tonight, he'll die. He has enough energy left in him to do one day's worth of farming labor. His reservation price—the minimum amount he'd be willing to take to work—is $1. At less than $1, he won't be able to buy food tonight. So, at less than $1 for a day's work, he decides it's not worth working, and would rather just spend his last living day watching the sunset.

Suppose in town there are 100 landowning farmers, each of whom is comfortable and rich. They could use Marvin's help on the farm, but they would be happy without it. Let's say Marvin's labor is worth $10 to each of them. If they pay him less than $10, they make a profit from his work. At $10 exactly, they are indifferent between him working for them and not working at all. At more than $10, his work is worth less to them than what they'd pay—they'd *lose* money on him. Imagine, if you want, that all of the farmers are complete sociopaths, with no sympathy for Marvin's plight. Suppose there are no other workers other than Marvin.

So, how much does Marvin get paid? You might think, "Well, Marvin is desperate for work and the farmers aren't desperate for workers. So, he'll get close to $1—his reservation price."

Nope. Rather, Marvin will get close to $10. Consider: Each farmer wants to pay Marvin the bare minimum $1. Suppose when one offers Marvin $1. The next farmer thinks, "Well, I can still make a giant $8.99 profit if I offer Marvin $1.01. So I'll offer him that." And so it goes—each farmer bids up the price of the others, right up to $9.99. Marvin may be desperate, but he has all the bargaining power. The competition between employers completely undermines their ability to take advantage of his desperation.

It works the other way as well. Suppose you desperately need your car fixed. If there were only one mechanic, he'd be able to charge you right up to your reservation point, right up until the point where you are indifferent between fixing the car or letting it stay broken. But when there are lots of mechanics, they bid the price down.

In competitive markets, there are lots of suppliers bidding against each other and lots of consumers bidding against each other. The result is that no one gets pushed around. No one gets to be in charge or take advantage of others. No one gets to decide the price. The needs of suppliers get balanced against the needs of consumers. Every possible mutually beneficial trade that can take place, does.

Market competition is competition to cooperate with others. We are trying to win the chance to cooperate with other people, which means we compete to offer better terms. They, in turn, have to do the same to win the chance to cooperate with us.

When you apply for a job, you compete against maybe a few hundred other applicants at most. This aspect of the market seems zero-sum, at least in the short term. When you get the job, they don't.

Still, even as you type your résumé on a computer, you're at the moment relying on the cooperation of tens of millions of unseen people who had a hand in producing that computer and supplying you with the electricity to run it.

Further, even though competing for, say, a particular job or particular contract involves a short-term, zero-sum competition with the other applicants, the system of competition as a whole is positive-sum. You are all much better off, and much richer, because you participate in a system that allows the kinds of competitions. Remember, the typical person living in a market society today is something like 20 times richer than her counterpart living in non-market societies in the past. In the short term, losing the competition for a desired job stinks. But alternative systems—where people don't compete for jobs but instead receive them by legal or cultural fiat—are systems where everyone is much worse off.

PROFIT IS A MEASURE OF VALUE ADDED

In a normal market, to make money means to make a profit. Let's be clear about what profit is.

As a seller, your profit is just your revenues minus cost. You make a profit as a seller when you value the money you make in the sale more than whatever you sold.

As a buyer, your profit is just whatever value you get from the thing you bought minus the cost of that thing. You make a profit as a buyer when you value the thing you acquire more than what you paid for it.

To illustrate what it would mean not to be motivated by profit, let's imagine you got to the grocery store, but want to make it a "non-profit" trip. You say to yourself, "Operating on a for-profit principle is bad, so I won't make any profits." What you'd have to do, then, is classify all the items into three types: 1) Items you value more than their price. 2) Items you value exactly as much as their price; you're indifferent between buying them or not. 3) Items you value less than their price. You'd

"non-profit"

rather keep your money than buy those items. To succeed in keeping your shopping trip "non-profit," you'd either have to buy nothing, or only buy items from lists 2 and 3, that is, items you are indifferent to or would prefer not to buy. If that sounds like absurd behavior, it is. But that's what it would mean to try to avoid "profit" in the economist's sense.

But what does your pursuit of profit do to others? Remember, in a competitive market, the price of goods and services is determined by the forces of supply and demand. In turn, these forces emerge from all market participants' individual knowledge and desires.

What this means, then, in a competitive market, for a company to make a profit selling something, they have to transform inputs that people value at one level into outputs people value at a higher level. *Profit is possible only if you create value for other people.* Profit means that from others' perspectives, you *added value* to the world. More strongly, the amount of profit you make *depends* upon the amount of value you add. Imagine you use $100 worth of inputs and transform that into something that people value at $200. That is, imagine that at $200, they are indifferent between buying your product or keeping the cash, but at less than $200, they prefer your product. In this situation, in a competitive market, you'll be able to sell the product for more than $100 but less than $200. Exactly what the price will be depends upon other factors. Still, the amount of value added sets an upper bound on your profit—you can make no more than $100 profit. However, imagine you'd turned that $100 of input into $1000 worth of output. In that case, you could make up to a $900 profit. The greater the value transformation—the more value you add—the higher profit you can possibly make. For that reason, then, we can take the profitability of an enterprise as a signal or a guide to how much good it's doing.

Americans tend to have this backwards. They tend to presume *some profit* is OK, but unusually high profit means the business must have done something wrong. As I'll discuss shortly, there is such a thing as profiting through ill-gotten gains. But such profit comes from cheating the market, not working within it. In a normal market, more profit for yourself means more good done for others.

In 2013, the Reason-Rupe surveys investigated Americans' beliefs about how much profit companies make. The results: Americans vastly overestimate the profitability of firms. They asked, "Just as a rough guess, what percent profit on each dollar of sales do you think the average company makes after taxes?" The *average* guess was 34%. The *median* guess was 30%.[10] In fact, the answer is closer to 7%.[11] Retail giant Walmart makes only around 1%–3%.[12]

As David Schmidtz and I pointed out in an earlier book:

> A corporation like Wal-Mart becomes the world's most profitable retailer not by making a fortune on any particular transaction, but by making tiny profits on billions of transactions. Virtually all of the gain from any given transaction between Wal-Mart and its customers goes to the customer, not the company.[13]

CAPITALISM IS BOTH A PROFIT-CREATING AND PROFIT-DESTROYING MACHINE

To make money in a properly functioning market, you have to transform inputs that other people value at one level to outputs they value at a higher level. To make extra-normal profits, you need to find ways to making even bigger transformations.

Economist Deirdre McCloskey describes an idea called the $500 bill theorem:

> Begin with economics. Take as an axiom of human behavior that people pick up $500 bills left on the sidewalk.
>
> If [so], then today there exists no sidewalk in the neighborhood of your house on which a $500 bill remains.
>
> Proof: By contradiction, if there had been a $500 bill lying there [before today], then according to the axiom someone would have picked it up . . . before today.[14]

In short, you shouldn't expect to find $500 bills just lying around on the sidewalk, waiting to be snatched up. If there were, someone would already have grabbed them.

What does this tell us about making money? Quite a bit, actually.

First, it tells you to be wary of anyone offering to sell you advice about how to make money. If a person offers advice on how to find a $500 bill on the sidewalk, for which he charges a nominal free, decline to pay for the advice. After all, if he really knew that, he would have already picked up the $500 bill. Take the advice only if for some reason you know the person can't get to the $500 bill himself. (Ask a management or marketing professor what the $500 bill theorem means about his own purported expertise. He'll like that.)

Second, it tells us that whenever there is a "sidewalk" with a $500 bill lying on it, then one of the following must be true:

1. By pure luck, no one has seen the bill yet, or the bill just landed a moment ago.
2. The bill is dirty and gross, or somehow difficult to pick up.
3. The sidewalk or the bill are hard to find and get to.

4. It takes unusual skill to pick up the bill.
5. The bill is stuck and no one has figured out how to pick it up.

Etc. Otherwise, again, someone would have picked up the bill already.

What this means, then, is that people who pick up the $500 bill—the ones who make the unusual, high profit—must either be really lucky, or have some talent, ability, knowledge, or willingness to do things others can't or won't do. If someone picks up $500 bills day after day, it's probably not luck. Everyone's lucky sometimes, but no one is lucky all the time.

The upshot of all this is that in order to make extra-normal profits, a firm can't just be lucky. It needs to innovate, to find some new way to solve a problem, or to identify and solve a problem others hadn't seen or understood. It has to find a way to solve problems and provide value *better* than others have. The logic of market is this: There aren't $500 bills out there for the taking. If you want to do better than average, you have to do something special.

Capitalism incentivizes people to make trades by only permitted mutually beneficial transactions. It encourages entrepreneurs to solve problems by offering them extra-normal profits for doing so. In these respects, markets are profit-creation machines.

But in another respect, markets are profit-destroyers. Consider: BMW realized people would enjoy—and want to buy—a sporty, small executive car with excellent handling. They created the 3-series and made lots of money. They effectively *created* a new market segment in the automobile industry.

But when they did so, they at the same time signaled to all their competitors: "Hey, there are $500 bills over here for the taking." And so their competitors started offering their own versions of that kind of car, some better than others. In doing so, they chipped away at BMW's ability to make extra-normal profits. The market rewarded BMW for innovating, and then incentivized and rewarded BMW's potential competitors to outdo BMW at its own game. To keep making profits, BMW cannot rest on its past success. It has to continually innovate and improve. As a result, a cheap Honda Fit today is a faster, more powerful car than a BMW 320i from 1978. But the 2019 BMW 340i is an even better car.

GOOD PROFIT, BAD PROFIT: PROTECTING CAPITALISM FROM THE CAPITALISTS

By allowing competition, capitalist markets constantly cut down firms' abilities to make extra-normal profits. For that reason, firm managers and owners themselves often hate market competition—and look for ways to stop it. They try to cheat the system, to get rules passed which entrench their companies and make it hard or impossible for competitors to arise. It turns out they get a lot of help in cheating from . . . well, from you!

Back in 1776, Adam Smith observed:

> People of the same trade seldom meet together, even for merriment and diversion, but the conversation ends in a conspiracy against the public, or in some contrivance to raise prices.[15]

Smith realized that businesspeople are rarely in favor of free trade. Free trade is a threat to any existing business, because the system of free trade is the very system that subjects businesses to competition. The system of free trade encourages and allows competitors to outdo you at your own product or service.

Instead, Smith realized, businesses are far more interested in winning special favors—such as government subsidies and protections. Businesses want the government to help them prevent customers from having the right to walk away. Smith saw that tradespeople, firms, corporations, and even not-for-profit organizations are constantly trying to form unions, petition for government monopoly rights, or otherwise rig the rules to raise their earnings far above what competitive markets would allow. As a result, we have to protect capitalism from the capitalists.

You might think, well, no problem. We'll just grant government the power to stop firms from rigging the game this way. In some cases, that may work. But in many cases that will backfire. The power to "stop firms from rigging the game" is also the power to rig the game. It's the very power the people who want to rig the game want to capture.

The power to regulate the economy for the public good is the same thing as the power to distribute favors. For example, occupational licensing laws nominally exist for the purpose of protecting the public—as a means of ensuring the public isn't harmed by incompetent producers. Maybe there's a case for requiring medical doctors to be licensed, though—contrary to what you might expect—the existing economics literature fails to find that licensing improves the quality of medical care.[16] Even medical licensing may be more about inflating doctors' wages and protecting them from competition than protecting the public.

But if that's too much for you, consider hairdressing instead. In ten states, to cut or braid hair requires you obtain a hairdresser or cosmetology license, which requires thousands of hours of classwork and training and costs tens of thousands of dollars in fees. In 15 other states and Washington, DC, you'll need to complete 450 hours of coursework. Most of the coursework is irrelevant.[17] There are similar licensing laws restricting a wide range of other jobs. If you go back to see why these rules were created, you usually find that they appeared during the Jim Crow era as a means of preventing lower-paid black tradespeople from competing with white people.[18] There is little evidence that these rules protect the public.[19] Instead, the laws mainly serve to reduce competition between suppliers and thus artificially inflate the earnings of current producers.

When we create government agencies with the power to control and manipulate the rules of the economic game, corporations and others will compete to lobby for, purchase, and control that very power. The more unscrupulous the corporation and the more they have at stake in controlling the agency, the more they will spend to get control. It is no accident that there is a set of revolving doors between government regulatory agencies and elite financial corporations, such as Goldman Sachs.

Americans are prejudiced against profit. They don't understand what it is. They think all profit is cheating.

But they're not entirely wrong. Some profit is. Some firms' profits do come at others' expense. Agricultural firm Archer Daniels Midland (ADM) makes some of its profits in an honest way, by providing services others want in a competitive market. But some of its profits come from rigging the game. It receives subsidies from government—which means the government taxes schmucks like you and me and hands the money to ADM. It benefits from laws requiring us to buy its products even when we don't want to—notice, for example, there is corn-based ethanol in your gasoline. The nominal—but mistaken—reason why the government mandates 10% ethanol in cars is that it's good for the environment (it isn't); the real reason is that corn producers have successfully lobbied for a regulation that serves their self-interest.[20] ADM also benefits from laws making imported sugar artificially expensive, thus inducing companies like Coca-Cola to use domestic corn syrup instead. For ADM—a company that excels at lobbying for favors—its rate of profit is indeed partly a measure of how much it has rigged the game.

This isn't to take back everything I've already argued. But we need to add another layer: To know whether a particular company's profits are good or bad, we need to know how it made its money. When a company makes a profit by getting government favors, through deception and fraud, or through coercion, it's bad profit. If it makes profit by making a deal with happy-to-trade Harry but pushing the costs onto inno-cent bystander Bob, then it's bad profit. But if it made it with-out fraud, deception, or coercion, without favors and without externalizing costs onto bystanders, then it's good profit. (As we saw earlier, that holds even when some of the people on the market start off poor and only have bad options.)

To get an overall assessment of the market, then, you want to know how much corruption there is. How much do firms collude with government for special favors? How competi-tive are markets? The more a realistic market approximates the economists' model of a competitive market, the more real-life profit is a sign of service. The more you have crony capital-ism, where success in the market depends upon getting favors from the government, the more real-life profit is a sign of exploitation.

This brings me to my final point. Many businesses lobby to rig the rules in their favor. Lobbyists and special interest groups often end up writing the very bills that regulate their industries.[21] We might ask, who's to blame for that? In addition to politicians, lobbyists, and special interest groups, you should probably blame yourself. When you vote for politicians who promise to regulate industry more and who promise to expand government's intervention in the economy, what you end up doing—though this was not your intention—is increase the value of rent seeking and make it easier for corporations and special interests to cheat the system. ("Rent seeking" refers to when people or corporations to change the background rules, regulations, or laws to benefit themselves at the expense of others.) When you vote for regulatory power with the goal of constraining ADM, what you do is help ADM cheat the system. ADM will capture a good deal of that power for its own benefit.

Measuring the degree of rent seeking in a country is extremely difficult. There are questions of definition: Do we measure the amount spent on rent seeking? The deadweight loss to the economy from rents? Something else? Further, even when we know what we want to measure, figuring out how to measure it is difficult.

Nevertheless, regardless of which measure we use, we still seem to find a strong correlation between the amount of government intrusion into an economy and the degree of corruption or rent seeking.

For instance, look at Figure 4.1. Each year, the Canadian think tank the Fraser Institute issues an index which scores various countries by how much economic freedom they have. In this case, I use their 2016 scores specifically for freedom from regulation. (A higher score indicates less regulation; a lower score indicates more.) I then plot that against Transparency

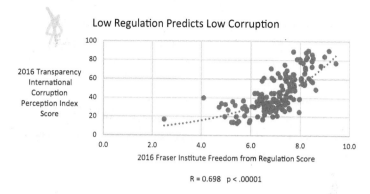

Figure 4.1 Freedom From Regulation and Freedom From Corruption

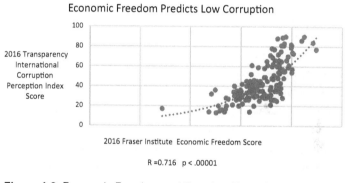

Figure 4.2 Economic Freedom and Freedom From Corruption

International's 2016 scores for how corrupt a country is perceived to be. (A higher score indicates less corruption; a low score indicates more.)

As you can see, the more regulation, the more corruption. The correlation between the two scores is .698, a very high correlation in the social sciences. You might notice, too, that the freest countries are significantly *above* the trend line.

Figure 4.2 does something similar, but this time shows countries' corruption perception index score plotted against overall economic freedom. Notice once again that the freer the country is, the less corrupt it is.

Regulation can and sometimes is used to reign in and protect the public from unscrupulous corporations. But the unscrupulous corporations themselves can benefit from carefully targeted regulations and rules. The more the government controls, the more opportunity there is to use government to one's own benefit. Amazon lobbied in favor of an Internet sales tax, a tax which disadvantage its competitor eBay. Released documents indicate that the now-defunct Enron lobbied for cap-and-trade regulations because they would hurt their competitor, coal, in favor of their own product, natural gas.[22] So, this is the essential paradox of regulation: To favor increasing regulation, you have to think the unorganized mass of consumers, taxpayers, and the common public will generally be more effective in lobbying for their interests than organized, highly motived special interest groups who keep offices in Washington, DC. You have to think that the people who enjoy concentrated benefits and can spread their costs onto others will be less effective than the masses who suffer from diffused costs.

Five

People believe it's not OK to make money because they mistakenly believe that profits are harmful. They presume that to make a profit means exploiting, ripping off, and harming others. On the contrary, as we saw, in a normal, well-functioning market, profitability is a sign that you are helping others. Sure, it's possible to make profits from cheating or rigging the system, but that's the exception to the rule, not the rule itself. It usually comes not from trading but from using political power to force people to trade with you. Indeed, many of the policies people support to try to *stop* that problem tend instead to make it worse.

Maybe now you understand that on a micro-level. Steve Jobs was richer than you because he made lots of trades with other willing customers, and you made far fewer. He had lots of trading partners and created a lot of value for others. You had fewer trading partners and created less. Whatever his personal flaws may have been, he became rich because he did far more to serve other people than any living kindergarten teacher, college professor, firefighter, soldier, or priest.

So perhaps we shouldn't be so suspicious of rich people. But, you might wonder, what about rich countries as a whole? In some countries—such as the US, Singapore, or the Netherlands—almost everyone is rich. Recall, as we discussed in Chapter

Two, even being at the so-called "poverty line" in the US puts you within the top quintile of people alive today and top 1% of people alive ever. In other countries, most people are genuinely poor.

Just as there are rich and poor people, there are rich and poor countries. Today, many people think or tend to assume that this disparity in the wealth of nations must be the result of ill-gotten gains or some nefarious process. Many people believe that the rich countries got rich *because* they hurt the poor countries. They might believe any of the following:

1. The reason some countries are rich and others are poor is that natural resources are unevenly distributed around the globe. The rich are rich because they have or had access to more or better resources than the poor countries did.
2. The reason some countries are rich and others are poor is that the rich countries (through conquest, colonialism, and empire) *extracted* resources from the poor countries.
3. The reason some countries are rich is that they benefitted a great deal from slavery.

If any of these claims are true, then maybe it's not quite so OK to be rich. Sure, we aren't responsible for the sins of the past. But if some countries are rich only because they were lucky enough to have good natural resources, that sure starts to sound unfair, or at least nothing to laud or admire. If they are rich because they plundered other countries, then perhaps we today are simply trading back and forth ill-gotten gains which properly belong to others.

If all or any of these three claims are true, it's not immediately clear what we should do about it. (As we'll see in the next chapter, "giving it back" is harder than it sounds.) But it sure would make it hard to celebrate our general level of wealth.

The thing is, economists have studied each of these three claims rigorously. It's true that the distribution of natural resources is uneven around the globe. Some countries have better "stuff" lying around than others. It's also true that many countries—including the UK, US, the Netherlands, Belgium, France, and Japan—engaged in imperialist plundering. It's also true that many countries, such as the US, have horrific legacies of slavery. None of that is under dispute. But—contrary to what your high school history teacher may have told you— economic analysis does not show that this is why some countries are rich and others poor. Quite the contrary.

Instead, the consensus in economics is that rich countries are rich because they have good institutions, while poor countries are poor because they have bad institutions.[1] The dominant view in economics is that sustained economic growth results from having good economic and political institutions.[2] Institutions, Nobel Laureate Douglas North writes, "are the rules of the game in a society or, more formally, are the humanly devised constraints that shape human interaction."[3] These rules can set the terms for social interaction in different ways, ranging from the harmful to the productive. The view that setting these terms in the most productive manner is the key to explaining growth has quickly become dominant in economics.[4] While no one thinks that institutions are all that matters, their importance is widely seen as paramount. As economist Dani Rodrik summarizes, the research shows "the quality of institutions trumps everything else."[5] In this chapter, I'll provide a crash course on this point.

THREE MISLEADING THOUGHT EXPERIMENTS

Let's start by considering three thought experiments.

These thought experiments are meant to elicit certain moral intuitions, judgments about right and wrong, and who owes what to whom. Many philosophers—and laypeople—think that the real world is or was analogous to these thought experiments. If so, then these will help clarify how to think about the real world.

> *Great-Grandma's Pie*: Great-grandma made a giant, delicious pie for her 195 great-grandchildren. However, for some reason she gave 80% of the pie to 20 of the great-grand-kids, and gave the other 175 only 20%.

When most people read this thought experiment, they think it's unfair that 20 kids get so much when the other 175 get so little. They conclude that perhaps those 20 kids should share their big slices with the other 175, to try to make things more equal. The 20 shouldn't be proud of their big slices. It's not like they did anything to deserve them.

The analogy, here, is supposed to be that the richest 20 countries are rich only because they had better natural resources than the other 175. If the analogy holds, then it's a mistake to gloat that American's wealth shows how great their country is. The US is just plain lucky: it has more "stuff" in its territory.

Here's another thought experiment:

> *Stolen Watch*: Your great-grandfather stole a watch from Bob's great-grandfather. He then left it to you. You're pretty sure that had your great-grandfather not stolen the watch, Bob's great-grandfather would have bequeathed it to Bob.

Most people react to this thought experiment by saying that while you didn't do anything wrong yourself, you still don't deserve that watch. That watch isn't a proper family heirloom— it's a mark of family shame. You should give the watch to Bob, to whom it properly belongs.

The analogy here is supposed to be that the richest countries are rich because in the past their citizens stole from the people in today's poor countries. The sun never set on the British Empire because the British Empire simultaneously plundered the Americas, India, the Middle East, much of Africa, and Australia. We're rich because our ancestors—or at least the people who lived here before we did—were a bunch of thieves. We're living off stolen goods and capital. No wonder the former colonies are mostly poor—they've been looted.

One more thought experiment:

> Great-Grandpa's Plantation: Your great-great-grandfather owned a massive cotton plantation on the Mississippi River. He sold everything and everyone before the Civil War. Since then, his money has been handed down to each subsequent generation, which has managed to stay rich through wise investments.

When most people read this thought experiment, they have a similar reaction to the Stolen Watch thought experiment. Sure, you personally aren't responsible for slavery. You didn't do anything wrong yourself. To stay rich over multiple generations, perhaps your family had to make various conscientious and smart choices which maintained the family fortune. Nevertheless, your family fortune ultimately originates in slavery. You can't take pride in your family's fortune and standing.

Some people think that this thought experiment is analogous to the entire United States. On their view, the United States is rich not because it had good institutions, but because it systematically exploited slaves.[6] Historian Edward Baptist asserts that "the returns from the cotton monopoly powered the modernization of the rest of the American economy."[7] He does not simply claim that slavery was an important institution, or that it explains *some* of the US's capital accumulation; he instead claims it's the *central cause* of American wealth.

I have no problem with these thought experiments qua thought experiments. I share most people's intuitions: the pie is misallocated, you should give the watch to Bob, the family money is shameful.

The problem is how thought experiments like these are used. It's true that resources are not evenly distributed among countries, that many rich countries engaged in imperialist plunder, and that slavery was a great evil. However, the field of economics has rigorously investigated these issues, and it turns out these things—resources, imperialism, and slavery—do not explain why the rich countries are rich. The thought experiments that grow out of the historical record are largely irrelevant to assessing the disparities between rich and poor countries.

THE GREAT ENRICHMENT AND THE GREAT DIVERGENCE

At one point, there were no rich countries; there were only poor countries. It used to be that everyone everywhere was poor. One place might have a slightly better harvest than the next, but the standard of living for the typical person everywhere was to be filthy, malnourished, deprived, and illiterate. For most of human history, there was only economic stagnation.

In 1821, Western Europe was slightly richer than most of the rest of the world, though it was still very poor. In 1821, the gap between Western Europe and the world average—in terms of GDP/capita—was only about 2 to 1. The gap between the very richest and very poorest countries was only about 5 to 1.[8]

If we go back further into history, the gap disappears. In 1000 AD, every person in every geographic region had roughly the same (poor) standard of living.[9]

Over the past few hundred years, though, things changed. Starting a few hundred years ago in England and the Netherlands, and then elsewhere, entire countries started getting richer and richer. Their rate of economic growth exceeded their population growth. The benefits of growth were widespread; average and common people got richer. Let's call this phenomenon the Great Enrichment.

The Great Enrichment was also the Great Divergence. When the Great Enrichment began, Western Europe and the Western European offshoots got richer faster than other countries. As a result, global inequality increased. The gap between the Western European standard of living and everyone else's standard of living increased. Today, the GDP/capita of rich countries such as Liechtenstein and Luxembourg is over 300 times larger than that of the some of the poorest countries, such as Burundi.[10] This doesn't mean Liechtensteiners consume 300 times what Burundians do. After all, GDP is fundamentally a measure of production or output, not consumption. But they certainly enjoy a much higher standard of living.

Economist Angus Maddison summarizes the trends:

> In the year 1000 the inter-regional spread was very narrow indeed. By 2003 all regions had increased their incomes,

but there was an 18:1 gap between the richest and poorest region, and a much wider inter-country spread.

One can also see the divergence between the 'west' (western Europe, US, Canada, Australia, New Zealand) and the rest of the world economy. Real per capita income in the west increased 2.8-fold between the year 1000 and 1820, and 20-fold from 1820 to 2003. In the rest of the world income rose much more slowly—slightly more than a quarter from 1000 to 1820 and seven-fold since then.[11]

Take a look at Figure 5.1, which shows the changes in GDP per capita from 1 AD to 2003 AD, using economist Angus Maddison's historical data. Figure 5.1 displays both the Great Enrichment and the Great Divergence.

I compress the time between 1 AD and 1500 AD because not much happened economically. The average standard of living around the world was low in 1 AD, fell a little in the 500s–600s,

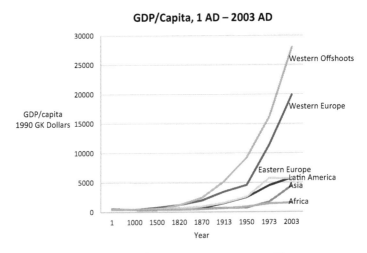

Figure 5.1 Regional GDP/capita changes over time[12]

and rose a little after. But the curve remains mostly flat until about 1500.

Notice that it was indeed a *Great Enrichment*. The Western European countries and the European offshoots (Canada, Australia, the US) grew richer, but so did everyone else.

It's not as though Europe grew richer to the same degree and at the same rate that other countries became poorer. If that had happened, that would suggest not a Great Enrichment, but a Great Reallocation or Great Redistribution. It would suggest that Europe's gains just were Africa's and Asia's losses, that there was a zero-sum reallocation of a fixed stock of wealth. However, that's not what we see. Instead, all countries started off poor. In the past 500 years, some countries became slightly richer, while others became vastly richer.

WHAT ECONOMISTS THINK:
THE INSTITUTIONAL THEORY

Adam Smith—the founder of modern economics—wrote the *The Wealth of Nations* in 1776, near the beginning of the Great Enrichment and Great Divergence. He looked around and realized that typical people in some European countries, such as England and the Netherlands, were significantly richer than people in other European countries, such as Spain or France. Given the conventional wisdom at the time, this was puzzling, since Spain and France had better natural resources and bigger empires. If natural resources and big empires are supposed to make countries rich, then why weren't France and Spain the richest countries?

Smith argued that what fundamentally explains the wealth of nations isn't natural resources. It certainly wasn't empire-building. (As we'll soon see, he demonstrated that imperialism was—to everyone's surprise—*bad* for the imperial country.) It wasn't that some countries had more virtuous, smarter, or superior people. Rather, it was that some countries had better *rules* than others. Some countries had institutions which encouraged and enabled their people to work in more efficient and productive ways, which as a result made everyone, even the poorest citizens, richer. Other countries—indeed, most countries at the time Smith was writing—had bad institutions. They were ruled by extractive elites, people who acquired money by extracting income from their people and by controlling their country's natural resources. These bad policies inhibited common people from being productive, which ensured the poor remained poor, as always.

Historians—who generally receive no training in economics or the social sciences more broadly—tend to *assume* that differences in wealth are explained by resources or conquest. But economists today instead agree with Smith's basic assessment. Rich countries are rich because they had institutions which encouraged growth; poor countries are poor because they had institutions which inhibited growth.

So, which institutions produce growth? Economists debate the fine details of these questions. Nevertheless, the basic consensus is that countries need A) robust protection of private property, B) open and free markets, C) the rule of law enforced, and D) stable and inclusive governments.[13] Countries, such as Switzerland, Canada, Denmark, Singapore, or Hong Kong, which adopt these institutions, nearly always become rich; the countries that lack these institutions nearly always remain poor.

Further, as countries move toward the A–D institutions, they become richer; when they move away from A–D, they become poorer.[14] For instance, economist Peter Leeson examined what happened to countries that become more capitalist or less capitalist (as measured by the Fraser Economic Freedom in the World Index) between 1980–2005. The countries that become more capitalist saw a 33% increase in real per-capita income, five extra years of life expectancy, about a year and a half of extra schooling per capita, and saw dramatic increases in how democratic they were. The countries that became less capitalist saw their income stagnate, life expectancy drop, and became less democratic.[15]

Each year, the Fraser Institute issues a report which ranks countries according to their commitment to economic freedom, taking account of such factors as access to sound money, free trade, ease of starting and doing business, ease of investing capital, the protection of property rights, and the degree of government control of or manipulation of the economy. The most economically free countries, according to the report, include Australia, New Zealand, Canada, and Switzerland. Each year, there is a strong correlation between how economically open and free a country is, and how happy, healthy, and wealthy its citizens are. For example, Figure 5.2 shows the relationship between GDP/capita and the Fraser Institute's economic freedom rating. Figure 5.3, which I take directly from James Gwartney, Robert Lawson, and Joshua Hall's *Economic Freedom of the World: 2016 Annual Report*, shows the relationship between economic freedom and the absolute level of income people at the bottom 10th percentile of income receive *before* any welfare payments or transfers.[16]

You can read the papers in the footnotes if you want to go through the rigorous statistical analysis needed to prove there is causation rather than mere correlation.[18] My goal here is to summarize what economists think and why.

Daron Acemoglu and James Robinson argue that the main difference between institutions that create growth or inhibit

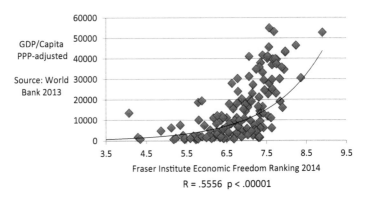

Figure 5.2 Economic freedom and GDP/capita

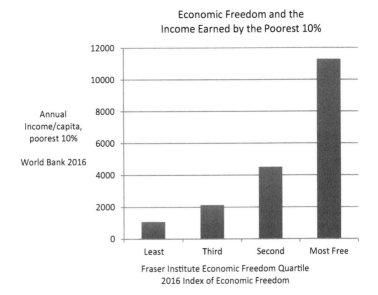

Figure 5.3 Economic freedom and income of the poorest 10%[17]

it concerns whether they tend to empower and incentivize people to work for one another's benefit, or whether they tend to empower and incentivize people to prey upon one another. What they call *inclusive* institutions, such as open markets and strong protections for private property, empower people across society. They incentivize and enable most people to invest long term and engage in mutually beneficial capital accumulation. In contrast, *extractive* institutions—such as dictatorships where the government owns the natural resources, or overly regulated economies where rent seekers rig the rules—empower only some, and thus tend to benefit only small groups of people at others' expense.

Acemoglu and Robinson explain:

> Inclusive [economic] institutions . . . are those that allow and encourage participation by the great mass of people in economic activities that make best use of their talents and skills and that enable individuals to make the choices they wish. To be inclusive, economic institutions must feature secure private property, an unbiased system of law, and a provision of public services that provides a level playing field in which people can exchange and contract; it must also permit the entry of new businesses and allow people to choose their careers.[19]

In contrast:

> Nations fail today because their extractive economic institutions do not create the incentives needed for people to save, invest, and innovate. Extractive political institutions support these economic institutions by cementing the power of those who benefit from the extraction. . . . In

many cases, as . . . in Argentina, Colombia, and Egypt, this failure takes the form of lack of sufficient economic activity, because the politicians are just too happy to extract resources or quash any type of independent economic activity that threatens themselves and the economic elites. In some extreme cases, as in Zimbabwe and Sierra Leone . . . extractive institutions pave the way for complete state failure, destroying not only law and order but also even the most basic economic incentives. The result is economic stagnation and—as the recent history of Angola, Cameroon, Chad, the Democratic Republic of Congo, Haiti, Liberia, Nepal, Sierra Leone, Sudan, and Zimbabwe illustrates—civil wars, mass displacements, famines, and epidemics, making many of these countries poorer today than they were in the 1960s.[20]

Be careful not to read the institutional theory of wealth as praising the rich countries or blaming the poor countries. It's often a historical accident or highly contingent outcome that certain countries stumbled upon good institutions while others got stuck in bad institutions. Smith and contemporary economists are not saying that England got rich because it had better people who in turn chose to create better institutions. Nor are they claiming that the people of Burundi chose to be ruled by extractive elites or did anything to deserve that fate.

The institutional theory is in some ways inspiring. It means getting rich doesn't require exploitation, good resources, or even good people. But in other ways, it's a bummer. While we know which institutions lead to prosperity and which institutions inhibit it, we don't know how to get the countries with bad institutions to change and adopt good institutions. We don't have a good theory of "social change." Further, the leaders of countries with bad institutions nearly always have a stake in maintaining those bad institutions—they make their living by exploiting their subjects or selling favors.

AGAINST THE RESOURCE THEORY

The Great-Grandma's Pie thought experiment makes it seem as though the reason some countries are rich and others poor is that the rich countries have more and better natural resources than the poor countries. Call this the Resource Theory. National borders are in some sense morally arbitrary, contingent, somewhat random outcomes of historical circumstance. But, the Resource Theory holds, through good historical luck, some countries end up with good resources and others bad. Those with good resources become rich and those with bad resources become poor. Philosophers, historians, and laypeople often just assume the Resource Theory is true.[21]

But economists have subjected the Resource Theory to rigorous empirical scrutiny, and the theory doesn't hold up. Economist David Weil summarizes the vast empirical literature in his widely-used textbook *Economic Growth*: "the effect of natural resources on income is weak at best."[22] Indeed, even the capacity to *discover* natural resources depends upon institutions; countries with market-oriented institutions are far better at discovering their natural resources than countries with non-market institutions.[23]

For instance, China after the 1950s was and remains poorer (in per capita income and other standard measures) than Singapore or Hong Kong, though the latter have almost no natural resources to speak of. The USSR remained poorer than the US throughout the 20th century, though the USSR had far better natural resources. North Korea remained poor while

South Korea became rich, though the North started with more industrial capacity and better mineral resources. In Adam Smith's time, the Netherlands and England were richer than France, though France had far better natural resources while the Netherlands was largely composed of land reclaimed from below sea-level. And so on.

Indeed, while natural resources can sometimes induce growth, they more frequently *inhibit* growth. Economists refer to this problem as the "resource curse": countries with a high concentration of easily extractable natural resources frequently suffer from economic stagnation.

There are competing theories of just why the resource curse exists, though to be more precise, these theories are largely compatible with each other and might be identifying joint causes. One theory holds that countries with abundant natural resources "do not develop the cultural attributes necessary for economic success."[24] Another theory is that countries which enjoy resource booms tend to just consume the sudden influx income in an unsustainable way. They don't develop capital, but eat away the extra income until it's gone. Another theory, the "Dutch Disease" theory, holds that a sudden abundance of resources leads to contractions in manufacturing.

Finally, the most popular theory today (or the theory thought to identify the most significant cause) is that when a country enjoys abundant resources, this encourages governments to act in destructive ways. Government officials can just extract resources for their own selfish ends and can afford to ignore or oppress their own people. Fighting over control of the resources can lead to civil war. Or, more simply, governments might create unsustainable welfare programs, programs they can only afford so long as resource commodity prices stay high.[25] See Venezuela for a recent example.

Regardless, while laypeople often accept the Resource Theory, economists largely reject it. The evidence goes the other way.

AGAINST THE IMPERIALIST THEORY

In the Stolen Watch thought experiment, you acquire a fancy watch because your grandfather stole it from someone else. Many laypeople, philosophers who write about global justice, and Marxism-indoctrinated historians assume that such theft explains global inequality. They think rich countries became rich by conquering parts of Africa, South America, and Asia. They developed capital because they stole resources from those countries. Today, rich countries remain rich because they inherited stolen wealth. Call this the Imperialist Theory of the Great Divergence.

For instance, philosopher Thomas Pogge says,

> [E]xisting radical inequality is deeply tainted by how it accumulated through one historical process that was deeply pervaded by enslavement, colonialism, even genocide. The rich are quick to point out that they cannot inherit their ancestor's sins. Indeed. But how can they then be entitled to the fruits of these sins: to their huge inherited advantage in power and wealth over the rest of the world?[26]

According to this view, imperialist resource extraction explains (or helps to explain) why first world countries became wealthy and how people in the developing world have become poor.

Now, even taken at face value, even before we do any rigorous economic analysis, the Imperialist Theory has some problems. First, if you look back at Figure 5.1, you see that after

1500, pretty much everyone is getting richer—or at worse, staying the same. If Europe's riches were merely the rest of the world's losses, we'd expect to see Europe get rich at the same rate the other places got poorer. We'd expect to see income moved around, but the total amount of income to remain about the same.

We don't see that. Instead we see *more* total income. Europe gets richer faster than others, but the others start getting richer too. So, anyone who believes in the Imperialist Theory needs to explain how European theft *created* wealth and made everyone richer. Perhaps the defender of the Imperialist Theory would hypothesize that the European powers were just tapping into previously unused resources in the colonies. They were cutting down forests or extracting unused gold.

The second problem, though, is that the historical facts don't quite line up with the Imperialist Thesis. For most of the imperial expansion period, Spain had the biggest empire, but it remained poorer than England or the UK. (As you'll soon see, this is no accident.) Why didn't Russia's enormous empire—full of natural resources—make Russia rich? The US and Germany got rich *first* and *then* acquired empires. Switzerland got rich without having any empire. After World War 2, Singapore, Hong Kong, Macau, and South Korea became rich, but they had no empires. Japan had an empire in the late 1800s through World War 2, but it didn't become rich until after it lost the war and its empire. The British abused and starved the Irish, but Ireland quadrupled its GDP/capita between 1970 and today, and is now much richer than the UK on a per capita basis.

Further, throughout history and all around the world, many countries have created massive empires. If imperialism is so lucrative and is the secret to growth, why didn't the Mongol,

Qing, Abbisad, Umayyad, Brazilian, Roman, Macedonian, Ottoman, Tibetan, Persian, Aztec, or countless other gigantic empires in the Americas, Europe, Asia, or Africa lead to an earlier Great Enrichment and Great Divergence? It's not as though Spain invented imperialism in 1492. It's not as though these earlier empires were especially nice and kind, or as if earlier empires didn't exploit their new subjects and extract resources. What gives?

Nevertheless, it is indeed true that the European powers (and later, Japan) engaged in widespread imperialist conquest. Some of the effects of imperialism are long-lasting. There is evidence that when Spain gave up its brutal, extractive empire, homegrown tyrants took up leadership and control of those same extractive institutions. There is evidence that some former colonies may indeed be worse off today as a result of being colonies yesterday.[27] Of course, the counterfactuals are hard to determine. What would the Congo be like today had Belgium never sent troops in? Would the area we call Brazil be richer and better run today if the British had conquered the land instead of Portugal, or if no one had ever conquered it?

At any rate, it's clear that starting in the 1400s, various European powers amassed large empires. They murdered, oppressed, and enslaved others, stole land, and extracted resources from their empires. The problem for the Imperialist Theory, though, is that these facts are insufficient to show Europe's wealth results from ill-gotten gains.

Adam Smith's *The Wealth of Nations* wasn't just a defense of the Institutional Theory. It was also the first sustained, rigorous economic critique of imperialism. Adam Smith carefully collected data about the value of the raw materials the European powers extracted from their empires. He carefully analyzed the various consequences of imperial trade restrictions and examined how much it cost the European powers to murder, pillage, and plunder. After all, these things cost lots of money. He estimates that the Seven Years War (1756–1763) cost Great Britain about 90 million pounds, while the 1739 war with the Spanish cost 40 million pounds.[28]

In short, The Wealth of Nations was a cost-benefit analysis of imperialism. In the end, Smith finds that the empires don't even pay for themselves. (Smith thinks it's a grievous moral error to ignore the welfare of the conquered peoples, but he shows that even if we do so, the empires still fail cost-benefit analysis.) Rather, Smith finds, the cost to the imperial powers in acquiring and maintaining their empires exceeded the value of the raw materials and other goods and service they received from the empires. Adam Smith argued instead that the leaders of Great Britain duped their subjects into thinking they had a profitable empire.[29] In fact, the British subjects were paying more in taxes to maintain the empire than they were getting back.

Indeed, Smith thinks the problems are even worse than that. Part of the problem is that imperial powers also encouraged inefficient production methods. For instance, Britain restricted Virginia's trade—they were only allowed to sell tobacco to England. The English might think they get a great deal on tobacco as a result, but on the contrary, it meant that Virginia didn't invest in more productive methods and didn't have an economy of scale. Colonial trade restriction hurt England along with everyone else.[30]

Imagine I pay $1000 for a gun, which I use to rob other people. But after all the robbing is done, I only collect $500. Sure, the robbery is evil. But it's no windfall. I, the robber, lost money on the robbery.

More recent and even more rigorous empirical work vindicates Smith's conclusion. Even if we focus narrowly on the economic interests of imperial powers (and ignore the harm they do to those they conquer), empires do not pay for themselves.[31]

One might wonder, then, if empires are such a bad deal, why did so many countries pursue imperialist policies? One reason could be that they were misinformed, just as most people are today. They didn't carefully pay attention to the data, and tended to just assume the math worked out.

But the deeper reason is that it's silly and naïve to compare an entire country to a great-grandfather stealing a watch or to an incompetent thief who pays more for his gun than he gains in theft.

Rather, nations are made up of different people with different levels of power and different interests. The benefits of the empire-building were concentrated among the politically well-connected few, such as weapons makers, certain monopoly trade companies, the military, and the kings and queens. The costs—which exceeded the benefits—were in turn passed onto and spread among the helpless, hapless many, among the taxpayers forced to pay for the wars, the conscripts forced to fight and die, and the consumers forced to pay what were in many cases artificially high prices.[32]

The Stolen Watch thought experiment is misleading because it gets the facts wrong. It's a bad metaphor for what really happened. In that thought experiment, you benefit from your great-grandfather's thieving ways. A more accurate replacement for the Stolen Watch thought experiment would go as follows:

Imperialist Queen

400 years ago, the Queen of Spain sent her armies to murder, enslave, and pillage the Americas. The Queen taxed

her subjects to pay for her wars, and forced many of them to die fighting those wars. The value of the raw materials they received from her empires was less than what they paid in taxes and in other costs. But the Queen was able to ignore and override her subjects' interests—she was queen, after all. As a result, the past citizens of Spain were poorer than they otherwise would have been. Perhaps—though it's harder to say—the Spanish citizens of today are poorer than they otherwise would have been, because their old queens and kings wasted so much of their capital and their people on costly empire-building.

Thomas Pogge assumes that the former imperial powers benefitted from their empires. So he assumes that our current wealth is ill-gotten. But the more accurate view is that imperialism benefit a select few people in the conquering countries, hurt most people in the conquering countries, and greatly harmed the people in the conquered countries.

AGAINST THE SLAVERY THEORY

American slavery was brutal and inhumane. All the criticisms of slavery are correct. I, for one, am no moral relativist; I don't excuse George Washington or Thomas Jefferson's slave-ownership because it was "normal" at the time. I think we should tear down Confederate statues.

The 1860 US Census estimated there were 31.4 million people living in the US at the time; 3.9 million were slaves.[33] On the eve of the Civil War, 12.4% of the population was held in bondage. In 2016 US dollars, the average price of a slave in 1860 was about $800, meaning these slaves were worth collectively about $3.1 billion in 2016 USD.[34] Economists Roger

Sansom and Richard Sutch estimate that about half the US South's wealth (not income, but wealth) in 1860 was in the form of slaves.[35]

That said, the degree to which slavery *explains* or accounts for the US's past or current economic prosperity is a complex, empirical question, which again requires sophisticated economic analysis. Fortunately, many economists have once again done such work.[36] The general consensus is that slavery was indeed economically profitable for slave-owners,[37] but it was not a particularly efficient form of production, nor does it explain why some countries are rich and others poor.

On the contrary, Nathan Nunn has carefully traced the economic effects of past slave-holding on long-term economic development, while measuring and correcting for other confounding factors. He finds there is a *negative correlation* between slave use and subsequent economic development. All things equal, the more a particular local economy, state, or country used the slaves *in the past*, the worse off it is *today*.[38] Numerous other economists have found the same results.[39]

In recent years, however, a number of historians in the "New History of Capitalism" movement have claimed that slavery is the main reason (or at least a major reason) why the US—and perhaps even much of the rest of the world—grew rich. Historians Sven Beckert, Walter Johnson, and Edward Baptist claim that slave-produced cotton explains the US's rapid economic growth and that it fueled and enabled industrialization and growth in Europe as well. Beckert in particular makes a number of fantastic claims about the importance of slave-produced cotton to the world economy, going so far as to assert that the industrial revolution was really caused by cheap labor from slavery.[40]

If they were right, this would be quite damning. But they're not right. Indeed, their work ranges from incompetent to outright dishonest.[41] Economists Alan Olmstead and Paul Rhode have published a systematic critique of their arguments.[42] I'm not going to recite all the New Historians of Capitalism's mistakes here. Instead, here, I'll examine the raw numbers and the biggest mistakes they make.

Beckert—author of *Empire of Cotton*—argues that slavery allowed Americans to exploit extraordinarily cheap labor. This in turn allowed capitalists to accumulate fantastic wealth, all surplus value extracted from the backs of slaves. But Beckert's basic argument doesn't check out. As Olmstead and Rhode point out,

> Among the most inexplicable claims in *Empire* is the assertion that antebellum American cotton planters "enjoyed access to large supplies of cheap labor—what the *American Cotton Planter* would call 'the cheapest and most available labor in the world.'" Beckert asserts that in India and Asia Minor, labor was scarcer than in the American South. The data suggest otherwise. Sources for northern India indicate that an Indian agricultural day laborer circa 1850 could be hired for the rough equivalent of $15.80 a year (300 work days).
>
> This is about one-quarter to one-half of the annual cost of food, housing, medical care, and clothing for American slaves. Estimates of annual maintenance costs of slaves circa 1850 range from about $30 to $61. Although he did not make an explicit comparison with American slave's subsistence, the abolitionist, James Cropper noted as much when he inquired: "In a densely peopled district, like that of Bengal, where wages are reduced to the lowest

rate of subsistence, where can be the profit or the motive for holding men in slavery?"[43]

In the end, it turns out that renting a slave to work your plantation for one year could cost *ten times* as much as hiring an Indian to grow cotton for you in India. Slaves weren't a particularly good deal and were not particularly low-cost labor.

American slaves were predominantly used to grow cotton. Cotton was no doubt an important crop to the South and to the textile industries in the US and UK. But we shouldn't exaggerate the value of cotton production. Olmstead and Rhode say,

> It was widely recognized that cotton was leading U.S. export in the antebellum period. But exports represented less than one-tenth of total income. . . . As the bottom line [of a graph in their article] makes clear, cotton exports were a very small share of national product—less than 5 percent over much of the antebellum period.[44]

While cotton was the single biggest US export in the antebellum period, exports overall (including cotton and all other exports) were worth less than a tenth of the total US income. A good estimate is that cotton constituted around 5% of US national product in the antebellum period.[45] In 1860, the US Census estimated the total value of all manufactured cotton goods produced in the US at about $120 million in 1860 USD, out of a total of $1.9 billion of estimated production.[46] In all, cotton represented around a twentieth of US manufacturing and agricultural output. Of course, slaves were used for other purposes, but then not all cotton was picked by slaves.

However, Edward Baptist does some hocus pocus in an attempt to show that relatively small numbers like these *really mean* that cotton completely dominated the US economy. He writes,

> here's a back-of-the-envelope accounting of cotton's role in the US economy in the era of slavery expansion. In 1836, the total amount of economic activity—the value of all the goods and services produced—in the United States was about $1.5 billion. Of this, the value of the cotton crop itself, total pounds multiplied by average price per pound—$77 million—was about 5 percent of that entire gross domestic product. This percentage might seem small, but after subsistence agriculture, cotton sales were the largest single source of value in the American economy. Even this number, however, barely begins to measure the goods and services directly generated by cotton production. *The freight of cotton to Liverpool by sea, insurance and interest paid on commercial credit—all would bring the total to more than $100 million (see Table 4.1).*
>
> Next come the second-order effects that comprised the goods and services necessary to produce cotton. There was the purchase of slaves—*perhaps $40 million in 1836 alone,* a year that made many memories of long marches forced on stolen people. Then there was the purchase of land, the cost of credit for such purchases, the pork and the corn bought at the river landings, the axes that the slaves used to clear land and the cloth they wore, even the luxury goods and other spending by the slaveholding families. *All of that probably added up to about $100 million more.*
>
> Third order effects, the hardest to calculate, included the money spent by millworkers and Illinois hog farmers, the wages paid to steamboat workers, and the revenues yielded by investments made with the profits of the

merchants, manufacturers, and slave traders who derived some or all of their income either directly or indirectly from the southwestern fields. These third order effects would also include the dollars spent and spent again in communities where cotton related trades made a significant impact another category of these effects is the value of foreign goods imported on credit sustained the opposite flow of cotton. *All these goods and services might have added up to $200 million.* Given the short term of most commercial credit in 1836, each dollar "imported" for cotton would be turned over about twice a year: $400 million. All told more than $600 million, or almost half of the economic activity in the United States in 1836, derived directly or indirectly from cotton produced by the million odd slaves—6 percent of the total US population—who in that year toiled in labor camps on slavery's frontier.[47]

Amazing. Somehow cotton—which US Census and other historical statistics say constitutes at most 5% of the antebellum economy—really accounts for half the US economy!

Keep in mind that this passage is absolutely central to the New History of Capitalism narrative. It's not enough for the them to say that cotton was 5% of US output and that much of the cotton was produced by slaves. Everyone accepts that. Instead, they are trying to argue that cotton *really* accounts for something like half of US economic output, and a great deal of British industrial output as well. They are trying to argue that cotton is the fuel that ran the industrial revolution and the bedrock upon which American capital accumulation was built. But the problem is that the passage above is utter nonsense.

Let's start with a relatively minor error. Baptist makes some mistakes in what goes in GDP and what doesn't. GDP measures final products. It does not include asset sales, such as the sale of land and slaves. US GDP obviously doesn't include British transport and insurance costs, which Baptist includes above.[48] So Baptist is already inflating his numbers, though I suspect non-economists will find this point nitpicky. (It's not—if he's going to count these asset sales but not others, it dramatically inflates his percentages.)

I italicized a few sentences in the quoted passage above; they are not italicized in the original. I want to call your attention to them. In each of these sentences, Baptist gives us an estimate for how much various goods or services may have been worth. But as economist Bradley Hansen notes, Baptist seems to have pulled these numbers out of thin air. He gives no data sources or evidence for them. For the "freight of cotton to Liverpool" number, he asks readers to refer to Table 4.1. But, as Hansen notes, "Table 4.1 does not provide, as one might assume, information about shipping and insurance. It does not even have any information at all for the year 1836."[49] It would be as if I wrote, "Baptist spends perhaps $10,000 a year on socks (see Figure 5.1)." You'll notice Figure 5.1 in this chapter contains no information about Baptist's sock purchasing habits.

It gets worse for Baptist. The hocus pocus he uses isn't just conjuring numbers from nowhere. Rather, he uses different magic to inflate these numbers, in order to conclude cotton explains about half of the US's output in 1836. Notice what Baptist does. He doesn't just take the value of the cotton that slaves produced. He *adds* to that number the value of all the inputs used into making that cotton.

But, as Olmstead and Rhode point out—and as we teach undergraduates in ECON 101—that's *double-counting*. To illustrate the mistake, suppose I bake a pie and sell it for $10. That shows up as $10 in GDP. But now suppose I said, "Well, I used

$4 of baking supplies and $4 worth of labor to bake that pie. So really that pie represents $18 of economic activity and output, the $8 value of the inputs and the $10 sale price." That's a mistake: the $8 value of the labor and the supplies was already included in the $10 sale number. Or, suppose I said, "My car sold for $60,000. But the engine is worth $5000. The tires are worth $3000. The front bumper is worth $2000. Etc. The workers who made the car got paid $10,000. It cost $400 in electricity to make it. Really, once you add up the value of all the parts of the car, and then add that to the value of the car itself, you see it's not really $60,000, but $120,000. That's the total output of the making that car." You can see the mistake. I double the value of the car because I double-counted.

That's precisely what Baptist does in the passage above, though—oddly—he doesn't even do it very well. He double-counts only *some* of inputs into cotton. So, he makes an elementary mistake in understanding how to measure output, but he also makes a mistake in making his mistake.

As Olmstead and Rhode summarize the problem:

> Baptist, for example, asserts that cotton production circa 1836 was valued at about $77 million and made up about "5 percent of the entire gross domestic product" (in line with Figure 5.2). But then by double counting and bad national product accounting, he boosts cotton's "role" to more than $600 million, "almost half of the economic activity of the United States in 1836." Here is his method: he adds the value of inputs used to produce cotton, though this double counts costs already subsumed in the cotton's price. He adds the estimated value of land and slave sales, though asset sales are not counted as a part of GDP. Further, he inexplicably adds

the "money spent by millworkers and Illinois hog farmers," and so on. If one extended this faulty methodology by summing the "roles" of cotton with a few other primary products, the amount would easily exceed 100 percent of GDP, which of course makes no sense.[50]

If, as Baptist does, we're going to count all inputs to a final product separately, plus all things the final product is connected to separately, then we'd get an even higher number than Baptist did. We'd conclude that slave-produced cotton was worth much more than 100% of US GDP in 1836. Impossible.

It gets worse. Baptist then tries to locate every economic activity in some way connected to or associated with cotton. He then adds various numbers-from-nowhere estimates of the values of these new "third-order" activities, and then adds these estimates to his final tally. From that, he concludes nearly half of all US production is based on slave-produced cotton.

To illustrate the error, imagine you have a widget-making machine which produces $1 billion a year in widgets. Suppose you discover that one $1 bolt in the machine was made by slave labor. What, then, is the contribution of slave labor to your widget making? Correct answer: $1. Baptist's answer, using the same logic as the quoted passage above: $1 billion. What Baptist is doing can be parodied like this: I paid $10 for lunch today, and I work at Georgetown University. Georgetown's total spending this year is around $620 million.[51] Using Baptist's logic, that means my $10 meal represents $620 million in output.

Actually, it gets even worse than that, as economist Michael Makovi pointed out to me. In the second paragraph of the Baptist quotation above, Baptist "estimates"/invents that in 1836, it cost $123 million to make all US cotton. He claims that cotton itself was directly worth $77 million. It takes another

$23 million to ship and insure it. But shipping and insurance are *costs*. In the second paragraph, he cites/makes up another $100 million in production costs. He says, "All of that added up to about $100 million more."

Profit, remember from Chapter 3, is revenue minus cost. So, by Baptist's own numbers, he should not conclude that cotton is tremendously profitable and somehow responsible for American prosperity. Rather, if cotton sold for $77 million but cost $123 million to make, then cotton production *lost* $46 million a year in value. By Baptist's own largely made-up numbers, he shouldn't be arguing that cotton explains the US's amazing prosperity. Rather, he should be left wondering how the US got rich *despite* the massive annual economic *devastation* cotton production unleashed.

There are a few other problems with the New History of Capitalism's central argument. For one, if slavery was—as these historians assert—such a great engine of prosperity for the US, then abolishing slavery should have been traumatic for the US economy. You'd expect to see a sharp drop in GDP when slavery is abolished in 1865. But check out Figure 5.4,

Figure. 5.4 US GDP/capita before and after the Civil War

which uses Maddison's historical GDP data. I marked 1865 with a vertical line, so you can see the US economy before and after slavery.

Notice there is no massive collapse. If I had just graphed GDP rather than GDP per capita, you wouldn't have seen collapse either. In constant 1990 dollars, US GDP steadily rises from $69 billion in 1860 to $98 billion in 1870 to $160 billion in 1880.[52]

Baptist, Beckert, or the other New Historians of Capitalism might respond that this all was because *slavery per se* wasn't the issue. Rather, it was the continual exploitation of cheap black labor, which continued even post-war despite the abolition of slavery. But during the 1861–1865 Civil War, almost *half* of all US-grown cotton was destroyed, and barely any of it was used.[53] If cotton was so important to the US economy, this should have produced at least a short-term economic collapse.

Yet another problem: During the Civil War, the Union imposed an embargo and blockade on the Confederacy, cutting off their ability to export cotton—and everyone else's ability to import it. This did not produce some massive or even minor economic collapse elsewhere. Rather, the rest of the world did what we'd expect: they bought cotton from Egypt and India and went on as usual.[54]

Let's be clear: Some people did indeed profit from slavery. Slaves were indeed exploited for profit. Slavery was indeed a horrific evil. Cotton was indeed a significant part of the US economy. But Beckert, Johnson, and Baptist have produced no evidence that slave-produced cotton or slavery in general explains the success of American or world capitalism, or explains why the US's standard of living and capital accumulation rose so quickly in the 1800s. Baptist's own numbers imply instead it was horribly unprofitable, with an annual loss rate over 50%. They haven't shown us that slavery explains American prosperity in the past or today. Baptist gives the most rigorous mathematical argument to this effect, but his argument rests on elementary accounting mistakes which my undergrads know not to make.

The most charitable interpretation of Baptist I can think of is this: He's thinking of the American antebellum economy as being like a giant machine, of which cotton is a vital part. He imagines that if you shut down cotton, you'd shut down something like half the machine. Now, he certainly hasn't come close to showing that. Cotton-users could have purchased cotton from India or elsewhere. They could have used other substitutes. They could have used factories for other products. In fact, only about 6%–7% of manufacturing production in 1860 was in some way cotton-based.

But even if we charitably grant him this machine analogy, he's still not thinking about this the right way. To illustrate, imagine I deflate the tires on your $100,000 Mercedes. Now you can't drive the car. But it would be a mistake to conclude that the air in the tires is therefore worth $100,000. The air is worth maybe $1.50—what it takes to replace it. You don't credit air with the total value of the Mercedes, even though the Mercedes needs air to run. You don't credit the cotton with half the value of the US economy, even if we grant for the sake of argument, as Baptist mistakenly asserts, that half the economy was like a machine that wouldn't run without cotton.

The New Historians of Capitalism are trying to damn American and world prosperity by arguing (unsuccessfully) that this prosperity comes from slave labor. But as historian Phillip Magness points out, this kind of genealogical tainting also works against the New Historians of Capitalism themselves. It turns out their arguments are nothing new. Rather, in the 1850s, Southern (and future) apologists for slavery made the very same argument. They claimed that cotton explained American and world prosperity and that industrial manufacturing around the world depended on slave-produced American cotton. They argued that abolishing slavery was, for that very reason, a bad idea. The New Historians of Capitalism wish to condemn capitalism because of slavery, but to do so, they parrot the same arguments the Confederate diplomats used to defend slavery.[55]

THE SINS OF THE PAST DON'T EXPLAIN THE PROSPERITY OF THE PRESENT

We tend to be suspicious of rich people or companies that make profits. We tend to presume that if someone else makes money, this must come at other people's expense. We see the world in zero-sum terms. In the last chapter, I argued that in market economies, this is usually a mistake. We tend to get rich by serving other people, not by taking from them.

On a more macro-level, though, many people worry that the difference between generally rich countries and generally poor countries comes down to historical injustice. The Resource Theory says that the rich countries lucked out and just happened to have good natural resources, while the poor countries had bad luck and just happened to have few natural resources. The Imperialist Theory says that the rich countries are rich because during the time of European colonialism, they plundered the poor countries. The Slavery Theory holds that the US, and perhaps a few of the US's big historical trading partners, grew rich because it practiced slavery. All three theories try to claim current and past prosperity result from morally arbitrary (in the case of the Resource Theory) or morally abominable (in the cases of the Imperialist and Slavery Theories) causes. But these three theories don't withstand scrutiny.

Instead, the consensus view in economics is that rich countries became rich because they had inclusive institutions which fostered and encouraged trade and investment in human capital, physical capital. The poor countries remained poor because they had dysfunctional institutions that impeded trade and such investments. None of this is to say that the people in the rich countries were better than the people in the poor countries. It's often a historical accident whether a country ended up with the good or bad institutions, and in general, leaders have tended to have a stake in implementing and perpetuating the bad institutions.

Note that I am not here making any claims about whether reparations are justifiable or not. That's a much more complicated question—and a topic for a different book. My point is more limited: The reason rich countries are rich today is not because of their past injustices, even though their pasts are indeed full of injustices.

The upshot of this is that just as you don't have to feel bad about making money or making a profit, so you don't have to feel bad about your country being rich. Making money doesn't require injustice, and countries becoming rich doesn't and didn't depend upon injustice. Yes, slavery and imperialism were horrific evils, and I am taking no stance here on what, if anything, we should do today in response to these historical evils. However, it's a mistake to claim English prosperity resulted from its empire, or that American prosperity resulted from its slaves.

Six

Over the past five chapters, I've argued first that it's OK to love money and want more of it. Money liberates us. It helps us live better, healthier, more authentic lives, with greater access to culture and knowledge from around the world. There's nothing inherently dirty about money, and there is little evidence that money corrupts us. I then argued it's OK to make money, so long as you make it by honest trade. In a normal market setting, to make a profit is a sign you are serving and helping others, not that you are hurting or exploiting them. Finally, I argued that the wealth the rich countries enjoy today is not generally the result of ill-gotten gains or unfair initial distributions of natural resources.

There's one last big idea to deal with: Once you have money, do you have to give it all away? Do we all owe a massive debt to society that we can never really repay? Or, is it wrong to be rich when so many people are poor?

In this chapter, I argue the answer to all three questions is no. Yes, you should help some, but at some point, you've done your share and have the prerogative to enjoy life.

DEBTS TO SOCIETY

Some people think we live in perpetual "debt to society." After all, life outside society would be nasty, poor, brutish, and short.

You live as well as you do only because you benefit from interacting with and trading with others, all in the context of institutions and norms that facilitate such beneficial interactions. You are born hungry and needy into a world that doesn't need you. In addition to your parents or guardians helping you, others pay taxes to subsidize your education. Whether you're a scientist or businessperson, you stand on the backs of giants and benefit from past discoveries of knowledge. You are rich in part because you benefit from past capital accumulation.

It's tempting to reflect on all this, and then conclude that however much money you make is a measure of how much you *take* from society. It's then tempting to conclude that you need to "pay it back."

It's true that we cannot repay our ancestors for whatever good they built and left us. We can and should feel grateful to them, but we cannot repay them. On the other hand, if all goes well, we'll do the same for our descendants. As I'll discuss at greater length next chapter, we can expect our descendants 100 years from now to be much richer than we are. We might not pay back people in the past, but we can at least pay it forward.

The other problem with the debts to society argument is that—at least if you're working a normal job in a decently competitive industry—when you get your paycheck, you aren't just *taking*. Go back and reread Chapter Three, about where profit comes from and how trade works. In a competitive market, if you take home $100,000 in income, then you also produced over $100,000 in value for other people. You gave back the same time you took. There's no unpaid debt there.

On this point, the philosopher David Schmidtz adds:

> If Jane participates in networks of mutual benefit, then by that very fact she is more or less doing her share to

constitute and sustain those networks. Admittedly, if Jane receives an average reward in a society like ours, she receives a package of staggering value (more than even [Thomas] Edison could have imagined a century ago). The fact that everyone's doing a little results in huge gains for nearly all makes it right for Jane to feel grateful to be part of the enterprise. Still, if everyone is doing a little, then doing a little is Jane's share.[1]

As Adam Smith said in the opening chapters of The Wealth of Nations, the gains from trade and from participating in networks of trade depend on the size of the market, the amount of specialization, and the technological level of the economy. In an economy like ours, a person can put in very little effort and receive a very high reward. (You get paid vastly more than a medieval peasant but you don't work much harder.) But that doesn't mean the person hasn't done her share. All of us working together the right way means a small share of work generates a high share of reward.

I work maybe 1000 fewer hours per year (and my work is far more enjoyable) than the average American did in 1870, but—adjusting for inflation—I make more per week than they did all year. It's again tempting to conclude I must be doing less for society than they did. But that's doesn't follow. Effort is a measure of the cost of the input, not the value of the output. The miracle of modern living is that my lower input produces more output today than their higher input in 1870. I put in less effort but I nevertheless contribute more. Same with you. You do a lot more to serve others than the average person in 1850 did despite not working as much or as hard.

Let's look more closely at the economics of earning a wage. In a competitive market, for-profit business firms hire workers in order to increase their own profit. Firms want to maximize their profit. They continue to hire additional workers so long as it's profitable to do so, that is, so long as hiring each additional worker increases the firm's revenue more than it increases its costs.[2] In a competitive market, neither the firm nor the workers have significant bargaining power; neither can push the other into a bad deal. Firms cannot offer wages far below the workers' marginal products, because other firms could then profit by outbidding them for those same workers. Workers cannot demand wages far above their marginal products, as other workers can then profit by underbidding them. Instead, in a competitive market, the equilibrium price of wages will tend to equal the worker's marginal product. If the marginal worker produces $15/hour of value, she'll make $15/hour. If she produces more, she'll make more; if she produces less, she'll make less.

So far, this is just an ECON 101 analysis of labor markets. More advanced questions in labor economics largely concern why real markets deviate in various ways from this basic model.[3] For example, some economists argue that workers get paid slightly less than their marginal products, because the ECON 101 model assumes perfect information and does not account for employer search costs.[4]

Here's why this matters for our purpose. As we saw in Chapter Four, when trading goods or services for money, you're giving back as you take, and people profit from what you give them while you profit from what you take. When it comes to work, the same principle holds. Your income may be a partial measure of what you get out of living and working with the rest of us. But it's also a partial measure of what you're contributing to others and the system of cooperation. You aren't incurring more debt by earning more income; you're rather simultaneously making others profit as you profit. You are paying as you go.

Schmidtz says, "any decent car mechanic does more for society by fixing cars than by paying taxes."[5] What he means is that we're already serving society just by showing up and doing our work. It's great to do extra, but we don't need to do extra to escape some incalculable debt.

We're not just serving our direct customers, either. Because we contribute to and maintain a mass division of labor, we're also simultaneously helping to create and maintain the background conditions of wealth, opportunity, and freedom. We create and maintain the extended system of cooperation that leads to all the benefits I described in Chapter One.

LIVING HIGH WHILE PEOPLE DIE

One of my relatives often proclaims—in between expensive vacations—that she chooses to live simply so that others may simply live. Many of my Facebook friends enjoy using their $800 smartphones to post pretty memes with the same message.

The messengers here may just be engaging in moral grandstanding,[6] but their *message* might still be right. Even if it's OK to make money, and even if it makes sense to want it, other people need it more than you.

Perhaps it's wrong to live high while people die. Perhaps it's wrong to consume so much luxury when so many people around the world live in extreme poverty or in desperation. Perhaps it's wrong to eat so much when others cannot eat.

The comedian Louis C. K. once built this point into his act:

> My life is really evil. There are people who are starving in the world, and I drive an Infiniti. That's really evil. . . .
> There are people who are like born and then they go, "Oh,

I'm hungry," and then they just die, and that's all they ever got to do. And, meanwhile, I'm in my car—boom boom, brrr!—like having a great time, and I sleep like a baby. . . . I could trade my Infiniti for like a really good car, like a nice Ford Focus . . . and I'd get back like twenty thousand dollars, and I could save hundreds of people from dying of starvation with that money. And every day, I don't do it.[7]

Maybe you don't drive an Infiniti, but this same reasoning almost certainly applies to you, even if you're a "poor college student." Anyone reading this book is likely among the top 20% or higher richest people in the world today, enjoying a standard of living far higher than most people today enjoy, let alone most people throughout history. You could consume fewer luxuries yourself and use the remaining money to help others. Should you?

It seems like you could free up money to help others by making small changes. Suppose you buy a Starbucks coffee every working day. If you work 260 days per year and pay an average of $4 per coffee, then you're spending $1040 a year on coffee. Instead, you could drink the free drip coffee your work provides in the break room, and then save about 30 people in the poorest regions of the world from preventable blindness.[8]

But why stop there? You could cancel your Netflix subscription, stop eating out, drink less alcohol, and take a less expensive local vacation. You could use a cheap Chromebook instead of a MacBook. You could buy a budget automobile—or bike to work. You could trim your wardrobe to a quarter of its size. You could spend your first two years at a community college. You could live at home instead of a dorm or apartment. With all the money you save, you could save a few lives.

Common-sense morality holds that you should give *some* money to help others. It holds that the more disposable income you have, the more you should give. However, it also holds that you don't have to make yourself poor to help those even poorer than you. At some point, you've done enough and have the prerogative to enjoy luxuries.

But some philosophers and religious leaders think the common-sense view is too lax. They think it's wrong to consume any luxury when other people are severely deprived. They think we should give all our extra money away.

Who's right? How would we know?

PETER SINGER'S BASIC ARGUMENT

In 1972, the philosopher Peter Singer wrote a famous paper, "Famine, Affluence, and Morality," which argued that our duties of charity or beneficence are far more stringent than common-sense morality holds. Singer argues that we should give away nearly all of our extra income and wealth to various charities.

Here is the basic form of Singer's argument:

1. "[S]uffering, and death from a lack of food, shelter, and medical care are bad."[9]
2. *The Singer Principle (Strong Version):* "[I]f it is in our power to prevent something bad from happening, without thereby sacrificing anything of comparable moral importance, we ought, morally, to do it."[10]
3. *The Empirical Premise:* It is within our power to prevent suffering and death from a lack of food, shelter, and medical care; we can donate large amounts of money to effective charities.

4. *Conclusion:* Therefore, we ought to donate large amounts of money to charity, or our governments.

Premises 1 and 2 are normative claims: they say what is good and bad, and what we ought to do. Premise 3 is an empirical claim: it says that we have the ability to stop suffering and death by donating to charity.

For now, let's just assume Singer is right and this is a sound argument. For the sake of argument, lets also assume you can easily identify an effective charity that will save lives. Now ask: *How much* would we have to give?

The Singer Principle, as stated, says that if we can prevent something bad from happening without sacrificing anything of *comparable* moral importance, we should do so.

That ends up implying that most of us living in rich, "first world" countries should give nearly all of our income and wealth away. Stopping someone from dying is more morally significant than you owning many extra T-shirts or an Xbox. Curing blindness is more important than you taking a vacation—even a *cheap* vacation. Stopping starvation is more important than your kids getting *any* Christmas or birthday presents.

So, if this argument is right, it means: no jewelry, no hobbies, no vacations, no eating out (unless it's cheaper than eating in), no fancy food, no philosophy books, no spending on anything you don't *strictly speaking need*. After all, almost everything you consume you don't need, and you could have instead used that money to cure blindness or stop starvation and disease.

Singer also offers a slightly less demanding version of this argument. In this less demanding version, he replaces the strong version of the Singer Principle with a weaker version:

The Singer Principle (Weak Version): If it is in our power to prevent something bad from happening without sacrificing anything of moral significance, then we ought, morally, to do it.[11]

This version of the Singer Principle allows you to consume *some* extra things you don't strictly speaking need. It's of *some* moral significance that, say, I give my kids birthday presents. So, I could buy them something small as a way of expressing affection and maintaining the family bond, even though strictly speaking these gifts are not *as significant* as saving a life. You can buy a used economy car, but not a luxury car. You can take a cheap vacation. And so on.

But even this weaker, less demanding version requires massive changes in how most of us live our lives. The strong version might require me to give away 60%–70% of my after-tax income, while the weaker version requires perhaps 35%.

I was a pre-doctoral research fellow at Brown University, an Ivy League school in Rhode Island, the first time I taught Singer's article. I remember a student shouted in agreement, "Yeah, soak the rich!"

I responded, "*You are the rich*. He's talking about *you*." The student newspaper had just published statistics showing that the median household income of the incoming first year undergraduate class was nearly $300,000. So, most of these students come from affluent backgrounds even by American standards.

But by the lights of Singer's argument, pretty much everyone in the US is rich. Check for yourself. Globalrichlist.com uses UN data to estimate where people stand in the distribution of income around the world. Suppose you make a paltry $15,000 a year in USD. Even after adjusting for the high cost of living here, you're still in the richest 8% of people alive. Are you sure you can't spare a little extra? As for me, Globalrichlist says the average person in Ghana would have to work around 2500 years to earn what I earn in one year.

That's the basic structure and basic upshot of Singer's argument. But so far, you might not be convinced. Let's see if Singer can change your mind.

THE DROWNING CHILD THOUGHT EXPERIMENT

Premise 2 of Singer's argument might already sound intuitive and plausible to you. But it leads to highly demanding conclusions most people are not prepared to endorse. So far, all the argument has really done is given us a dilemma: either reject premise 2 or accept the conclusion (4).

Singer has a powerful thought experiment that appears to give us strong grounds for accepting at least the *weak version* of the Singer Principle:

> if I am walking past a shallow pond and see a child drowning in it, I ought to wade in and pull the child out. This will mean getting my clothes muddy, but this is insignificant, while the death of the child would presumably be a very bad thing.[12]

Let's rewrite this thought experiment into an even clearer form, one which puts an exact price on the sacrifice you'd have to make to save the drowning child:

One Drowning Child

You are walking in the park, when you see a child drowning in a pool. You can easily reach in and save the child, though doing so will cause you to drop $3337.06. which will blow away in the wind and be lost forever. Are you obligated to save the child?

Note: I realize $3337.06 is a weirdly specific number for a thought experiment. I use this because as of the time I write this, Business Insider claims this is the lowest amount you could spend on a charity with a guarantee you'll actually save an individual life.[13]

Nearly everyone responds *yes, you are obligated to save the child.* They do not simply conclude it would be kind to save the child. Rather, they say you must save the child and it would be wrong not to do so. They might allow that if you desperately needed the $3337.06 to save yourself or your loved ones, then you might be excused from saving the drowning child. But otherwise, if you were going to spend that $3337.06 on stuff you don't strictly speaking need, they conclude you must save the child.

You might object, "Why is it my responsibility? Shouldn't the parents or the child's guardian's rescue it?" Singer responds that sure, they should. But suppose you saw a child drowning while the parents or other bystanders stood by, doing nothing. You wouldn't conclude that this excuses you from rescuing the child. You'd conclude you should save her, even though other people should have saved her first.

Singer then asks: Since you believe you ought to save the hypothetical drowning child, even if it costs you $3337.06, then why not save a real child right now for $3337.06? Consider this variation of One Drowning Child:

One Starving Child

There is a child starving on the other side of the world. You could easily save his life, but only if you decide not to take a $3337.06 vacation and instead donate the money to a charity.

There is a clear *psychological* difference between this case and the last, which explains why we behave differently. When we actually see a child drowning, we immediately sympathize with the child and drop everything to save her. In contrast, reading about children suffering does not elicit the same sympathetic response. Statistics don't make our hearts hurt. We react to things in front of us differently from things we simply know about. That's because, as I argued in Chapter Four, our moral psychology evolved for face-to-face interaction within small groups, not for a world like ours where we can cooperate with or affect strangers across the globe.

But, Singer says, while there may be a *psychological* difference between the two cases, there is no *moral* difference. If we're committed to saving the drowning child we see, we should also be committed to saving any unseen dying children.

You might be worried that giving $3337.06 to charity won't do any good. When you pull a child out of a pool, you know you saved her. When you write a check to a charity, maybe all you did was buy a laptop for some administrator. Lots of charitable giving is useless, and some is worse than useless.

That's a reasonable worry, Singer says. But you can do research to determine which charities work and which don't. You could read philosopher William MacAskill's wonderful book *Doing Good Better* for excellent advice on how to assess effective versus ineffective and even harmful forms of charity. GiveWell.org researches effectiveness; each year GiveWell publishes a list of the most life-years-extended-per-buck charities. It's easy today to find good charities. Maybe you're a college student who can't afford a $3337 donation. But you can afford to deworm dozens of children, which will greatly improve their physical and mental development and extend their lifespans. You can afford to cure a few people of blindness. Whoever you are, you could do far more to help people through charity than you do.

DOES ONE DROWNING CHILD SUPPORT THE SINGER PRINCIPLE?

In One Drowning Child or One Starving Child, you save a life, but then carry on with your life. You lose $3337.06, but you aren't destitute.

However, the Singer Principle does not say you must save one kid, and then you're done. Remember, even the weaker form of the principle is highly demanding. The Singer Principle dictates that you must keep saving more and more kids, right up until the point where saving them would sacrifice something of moral significance (on the weak version of his principle) or comparable moral worth (on the strong version).

So, what Singer seems to imagine is not that you encounter one drowning child, and then save it. He seems to be imaging that you come across drowning child after drowning child. As soon as you save one, you find—or at least know about—another you can save.

That's a problem for Singer's argument. Most of us judge we must save at least one child. But it's unclear that because you intuitively judge that you must save one child, that commits you to then saving every additional child you see. If you judge— as most people and I do—that you must save the child, this doesn't show that you are implicitly committed to the Singer Principle. It's not obvious that the Singer Principle explains your intuitions in these cases.

To illustrate, consider this variation of the drowning child example:

Many Drowning Children

> You are walking in the park, when you see a giant pool filled with drowning children. New children are constantly falling in every moment. You can choose to try to save some of the children. Each time you save a child, it will cost you $3337.06. The children you save will for the most part remain saved, though some might fall back in. However, no matter how many you save, there will always be more who fall in and are just about to drown. You can spend your entire waking life pulling children out of pools.

This new thought experiment is more analogous to the real world than the previous two, which Singer relied on. So, whatever your intuition is here tells you more about what you implicitly believe you must do in response to drowning children.

What Many Drowning Children does is *iterate* One Drowning Child over and over. Singer assumes that because you think it's obligatory to save the child in One Drowning Child, then you'll have the same judgment if we iterate the thought experiment again and again. But, in fact, you probably don't. You probably think that you have to save the first child, but at some point, you can move on and live your life, even though children will die.

Ask, in Many Drowning Children, how many children are you obligated to save? If you think: I must keep saving kids—at $3337.06 a child—right until the point I would sacrifice something of high moral significance, then you are indeed committed to the Singer Principle. And you should, by your own uncovered moral judgments, give away most of your income.

You might instead believe, going along with more common-sense, conventional morality, that you ought to save some children, but at some point, you are permitted to get on with your life, even though you know more children will die. Analogously, you would then judge that you ought to give *some* to charity—and perhaps much more than you actually give—but at some point, even though you could give more, you've given enough, and get on with enjoying your life. You should help people, but you aren't obligated to live in complete simplicity so that others may simply live. You may live high while others die.

Singer says distance doesn't matter. You agree that if you come across a kid drowning, you'd better save them, unless you have a damn good excuse. So, he asks, what difference does it make if you *know* a kid is drowning somewhere, but not here, where you are? You know you could identify the drowning kids with a little work. You know with a little more work you could find ways to stop them from drowning—or dying of other means—for a few thousand dollars.

But, contrary to Singer, perhaps it does make a difference whether you *encounter* the problem or not. Consider two moral "policies" you might adopt:

- *Save One*: I will save the first drowning child I come across.
- *Save Them All*: I will save all the dying children in the world I possibly can before I die.

On their face, Save One and Save Them All are very different policies. Singer wants to show us that if we're committed to Save One, then we're committed to Save Them All. So far, though, he hasn't given us a strong reason to think that.

What this shows is that the One Drowning Child thought experiment does not quite do the work Singer needs it to do to get us to believe his principle.

HOW SINGER MIGHT RESPOND

I doubt Singer would be much impressed by this criticism. Instead, he might claim I have misconstrued his argument. He's sort of right, but only sort of.

To be clear, in "Famine, Affluence, and Morality," he never says that the reason you should endorse the Singer Principle is that it best explains your intuitions in One Drowning Child. He does not say, "If you agree with me that you must save the drowning kid, then you are thereby committed to the Singer Principle."

Rather, he says that Drowning Child is simply an instance of or an illustration of the Singer Principle. He uses it to explain how the principle works, not to show us that the principle is true.

That's Singer's self-understanding and how he explicitly frames his argument. Fair enough.

However, I don't think that much helps Singer. Even though Singer doesn't think his argument relies upon generalizing or iterating the Drowning Child thought experiment, the Drowning Child thought experiments nevertheless do most of their work for him. People find Singer persuasive because they think they cannot consistently hold A) that they must save the one drowning child, and B) that they are permitted to refrain from donating most of their income to charity. Singer himself recognizes the power of the Drowning Child thought experiment. He begins his popular book *The Life You Can Save* by invoking it, and then uses it to try to get readers to endorse the Singer Principle.[14]

So, insofar as people find Singer potentially convincing, here's what really happens. Readers agree that they are obligated to save one drowning child. Singer then tries to show readers that distance doesn't matter, so they should agree that they must save at least one dying child they don't encounter. So far, so good, perhaps. But then he tries to argue, again on pain of inconsistency, that if they admit they must save one life, they are committed to saving lives up until the point of serious self-sacrifice. This last step, however, doesn't quite work.

WHAT YOU DO WHEN YOU BUY LUXURIES OR INVEST

Some people are rich and live in rich countries. They're the people Singer thinks have an obligation to help. Others are poor, and there are still entire countries where almost everyone is poor. These are the people Singer thinks we have strong duties to help.

But it's worth stopping and thinking about how it came about that some are rich—and thus in a position to give—in the first place? After all, in 1800 AD, 95% of the world was destitute, living in what we'd now consider extreme poverty. In 1900 AD, about 75% were. Now, maybe 9% of people are, while nine out of ten people live above extreme poverty. In 1950, Japan, South Korea, Hong Kong, Singapore, and Taiwan were very poor. Singer would have said we have duties to give our extra income to their citizens. In 2020, Japan, South Korea, Hong Kong, Singapore, and Taiwan are very rich—indeed, the average person in Singapore is now richer than the average American. Singer today would say the Japanese, Koreans, etc., have duties to give their extra income away. But we should ask, how did the people in these recently poor countries go from being the kinds of people Singer thinks ought to be helped to the kinds of people Singer thinks ought to give help?

The answer: It's not as though Japan and Korea went from being full of people who need help to people who can help because anyone listened to Singer. Rather, they became rich precisely because people ignored Singer's advice. Over the past 60 years, people in already rich countries bought toys, transistor radios, stereos, video game consoles, VCRs, DVD players, Blu-ray players, smartphones, automobiles, electronics, and a wide range of other morally insignificant luxury goods they didn't need from these countries. The result wasn't that their people starved while their economies went on making useless trinkets. The result was instead that their people were liberated from poverty and joined the ranks of the rich.

Today, China is starting to move toward being a middle-income country. Some parts of China are quite rich, while others remain poor. But it was only when China partly liberalized, and when Americans and others started buying so many unneeded, morally insignificant luxury goods from China, that China finally started to escape extreme poverty.

There are a few historical examples of countries avoiding sudden collapse or utter chaos thanks to handouts from wealthier countries, but there are no examples of countries having sustained, poverty-ending growth as a result of such handouts. Rather, all of the rich countries grew rich by participating in the world market economy, by producing things others wanted at prices they could afford to pay. Historically, the thing that eradicates extreme destitution is not throwing money at destitution, but throwing money into the very forms of commerce Singer wants to eliminate and regards as morally wrong.

INVESTING VS. CHARITY

A similar point holds for investing money, rather than spending it. When you save cash in a bank account or buy stocks, you don't simply sit back and eat the profits. That money gets used—to fund college loans, business loans, capital development, infrastructure development, personal loans, and a whole host of other growth-creating activities.

Of course, not every investment succeeds. But there is a real trade-off between charity and investment. With $3337.06 given to the right charity, you can save a life today and do an amazing amount of good. By investing that same $3337.06, you can—let's say with no additional contributions and with a mild 5% annualized rate of return—create nearly $450,000 in value 100 years from now. That money can save a life today or, better yet, make it so that people in the future don't need to be saved.

I don't say this to suggest you should never help someone now and always invest instead. I don't say this to suggest the contrary position either. I say this to acknowledge there is a genuine moral trade-off here. The world doesn't play fair; it makes us choose between feeding the hungry today or ensuring people can feed themselves tomorrow.

DON'T SHUT DOWN THE WORLD ECONOMY

We face a dilemma: Save people now or invest and trade in ways that make it so people don't need to be saved? Either way, we lose something of value. What should any one of us do?

I don't think the answer is let everyone starve, and instead invest everything. But the answer is clearly not this: shut down the world economy and spend everything meeting others' needs. That's not the answer because it would fail on its own terms.

To illustrate, imagine we're living in a subsistence level agricultural economy. The crop fails. People starve. They start eyeing the silos where we keep the seed corn—the corn we've stored not for eating, but to plant crops next year. Someone suggests we eat that.

If we eat the seed corn today, we don't starve today. We make it through the winter. But come spring, we have nothing to plant. So, we starve next fall rather than this fall. The lesson: You don't eat your seed corn.

That's the terrible logic of seed corn. It holds even for advanced, industrial economies. The rich countries full of rich people are rich because in the past, their citizens engaged in capital accumulation and sustainable patterns of commerce and trade. To some degree, though, we could liquidate much of that capital, and use it instead to feed the starving and cure the sick. Should we?

Peter Singer acknowledges the danger. He says that there is a limit to how much we should slow down the economy to meet others' needs. Our ability to give depends upon our ability to be in a position to give. It could turn out that if we gave away, year after year, say, 50% of GDP, the economy would be so devastated that we'd end up giving less than if we gave away 25%.

Princeton University, where Singer works, has a $25 billion endowment.[15] Princeton uses maybe 4%–5% of that each year for operating funds, but keeps the rest invested, where they get a return over 5%. As a result, Princeton's spending is mostly sustainable—they grow more than they spend. Suppose Princeton decided to eat its seed corn: it decides to liquidate all $25 billion and spend all of it this year, trying to deliver the best education and research it can. With $25 billion in operating revenues, no doubt Princeton would have one amazing year. But then next year comes, and the money is gone. This year's amazing output means no output next year—or any year after. Princeton burns away.

The philosopher Peter Unger takes an even more extreme position than Peter Singer. He asks us to imagine

> whenever well-off folks learn of people in great need, they promptly move to meet the need, almost no matter what the financial cost. So, at this later date, the basic needs of almost all the world's people will be met almost all the time. . . . What's more, should any of these descendants find herself facing such preventable suffering as now actually obtains, she'd devote almost all her energy and resources toward lessening the suffering.[16]

The philosopher and economist David Schmidtz responds that he doubts that Unger's thought experiment is "even coherent":[17]

> It has the following logic. The productive output of the western world is put up for grabs. A world-wide competition ensues. And the way for a country's leaders to win the competition for that output is to have a population that seems to need it more than anyone else. But if we devote almost all our energy and resources to meeting such need, *then how do we get to be so well off?* Where does Unger think prosperity comes from in the first place?

Schmidtz goes on to ask you to imagine we lived by Unger's precept. No one goes to the movies or eats out—surely these are luxuries we don't need. So those places close and their employees have to seek work elsewhere. They won't find it at other retail stores—most of those will close, since we're no longer buying anything we don't absolutely need. The factories close for the same reason. Soon most of our community—working in fields and businesses people don't strictly speaking need—is out of work. They don't repay any of their loans, and the banks close. Maybe for one year we send lots of money to stop starvation in Yemen, but then come next year, we've become refugees too.[18]

WHY HAVEN'T WE ALREADY SAVED THE WORLD?

Philosophers and laypeople see that some people live high while others die. They see that some people have plenty and some not enough. It seems like it should be *easy* to fix the problem. It's just a simple problem of reallocating wealth and income better.

Like most economists, Nobel Laureate economist Angus Deaton is skeptical that fixing world poverty is that easy. However, he says, if all it takes is a simple transfer, then curing world poverty would require barely anything from us. It doesn't require that the West impoverishes itself to feed the rest. He says,

> One of the stunning facts about global poverty is how little it would take to fix it, at least if we could magically transfer money into the bank accounts of the world's poor. In 2008, there were about 800 million people in the world living on less than $1.00 a day. On average, each of these people is "short" about $0.28 a day. . . . We could make

up that shortfall with less than a quarter billion dollars a day. . . . Taking . . . into account [differences in purchasing power in poor countries], . . . world poverty could be eliminated if every American adult donated $0.30 a day; or, if we could build a coalition of the willing from all the adults of Britain, France, Germany, and Japan, each would need to give only $0.15 a day.[19]

It seems so easy. If we could just magically transfer 15 cents a day—$54.75/year—from every adult in the US, UK, France, and Germany to every person living in extreme poverty, extreme poverty would disappear.

Maybe it is that easy, and it turns out we're just incredibly selfish or stupid. But then—at least among the 25% or so of Americans who itemize their tax returns—the average American is already giving over $1000 to charity every year.[20] So perhaps we're just stupid. We have the will to fix world poverty, but for some reason we spend the money badly.

Deaton says the mathematics is misleading. After World War 2, the US and various European powers provided hundreds of billion in foreign aid to various poor countries.[21] But the results were bad:

> Growth *decreased* steadily while aid *increased* steadily. When aid fell off, after the end of the Cold War, growth picked up; the end of the Cold War took away one of the main rationales for aid to Africa, and African growth rebounded. . . . [A] more accurate punchline would be "the Cold War is over, and Africa won," because the West reduced aid.[22]

In a comprehensive review of the existing empirical literature on foreign aid, Hristos Doucouliagos and Martin Paldam conclude, "after 40 years of development aid, the evidence indicates that aid has not been effective."[23] Overall, the research generally finds that aid is more likely to hurt than to help. In general, economists find that aid does a small amount of good in countries that already have good institutions, but tends to make things worse in countries with bad institutions.[24] But this also means that the countries with the neediest people are also the least likely to benefit from aid.

Acemoglu and Robinson explain why:

> The idea that rich Western countries should provide large amounts of "development aid" in order to solve the problem of [world] poverty . . . is based on an incorrect understanding of what causes poverty. Countries such as Afghanistan are poor because of their extractive institutions—which result in a lack of property rights, law and order, or well-functioning legal systems and the stifling domination of national and, more often, local elites over political and economic life. The same institutional problems mean that foreign aid will be ineffective, as it will be plundered and is unlikely to be delivered where it is supposed to go. In the worst-case scenario, it will prop up the regimes that are the very root of the problems of those societies.[25]

These countries are government by elites who make a living (and stay in power) by extracting resources from their countries and people.

When rulers make a living by extracting resources and income from their subjects, sending more money means increasing the potential rewards of being in power. Foreign aid helps bad governments persist without gaining the support of their citizens. It tends to encourage factions within those countries to compete for power to gain control of the incoming aid. Targeting aid to the people who need it sounds easy from the philosopher's armchair, but in the real world, it isn't.

Countries become rich when they have good institutions, institutions which facilitate cooperation, discourage looting, and encourage long-term investments in human and physical capital. We don't know how to induce countries to adopt such institutions. We do know that throwing billions of dollars at them has never worked.

THE STATUS QUO

The common-sense view of charity is that you should give some to charity, in proportion to how much extra you have. There's no fine line where you've done enough. Still, at some point you've done enough, and any extra you give is admirable, if not required. Singer tried to persuade us to adopt a more demanding view, but this argument didn't succeed. That doesn't quite vindicate the common-sense view, but it does mean that we have no obvious reason to depart from it.

Further, contrary to what some moralists assume, buying "stuff we don't need" has a far better track record of alleviating poverty than giving things way. This doesn't mean we should avoid charity altogether. Certain targeted forms of charity can do significant good.

Still, we face a constant dilemma: investing our extra income in the long-term has far more poverty-fighting power than charity does today. Buying "stuff we don't need" has more long-term poverty-fighting power too. But there are people who need our help today. Whether we choose to invest, consume, or give, something will be lost.

Don't read any of this as a defense of the status quo. On the contrary, I suspect you should give more than you do, if not as much as Singer recommends. I also think helping the poor requires some radical changes—in particular, making it as easy to move from Burundi to the US as it is to move from Maryland to Virginia. The economics of immigration show this would benefit both global poor—and us, too—far more than any international aid or charity could hope to do. But that's for another book.[26]

Seven

Here's what we've covered so far: It's OK to love money. It's OK to make money. It's OK that your country is rich. It's OK to keep much of it rather than give it all away.

In this chapter, I'll address two remaining doubts or worries about money and riches:

1. It still seems slimy and sleazy to flaunt your riches or to be interested in luxury goods.
2. Isn't there a point where people just have enough? How much better can we eat, really? At some point, shouldn't we stop growing the economy and focus on higher callings?

In the last chapter, we saw that Peter Singer regards almost everything you own as a luxury good, because strictly-speaking you don't need that stuff. In this chapter, though, I want to focus on the more conventional idea of a luxury good. A Rolex is a luxury watch; a Timex is not. A BMW 7-series is a luxury car; a Chevy Cruze is not. Balmain makes luxury jeans; Wrangler does not. Hermes makes luxury belts; Marino Avenue does not. A Fender American Elite Stratocaster is a luxury guitar; a Squier Bullet Strat is not.

The problem with luxury goods—in this sense—is that they are designed to be exclusive. Their appeal is not simply that they are higher quality (indeed, sometimes luxury items are not), but that they remain out of the reach of the many. Such luxury goods allocate status—but they raise some people up by pushing others down.

The problem with allocating status is that it's often a "zero-sum" game. Everyone in the world can become richer, smarter, healthier, or more beautiful in absolute terms. But status is often about *rank*—about how we compare to each other. If I buy luxury goods you can't afford, I might be trying to signal that I'm thereby *better* than you.

That seems rather repulsive, even though we all do this kind of thing. I suspect a great deal of people's aversion to wealth comes from envy and resentment. (Indeed, philosophers often wonder whether egalitarian philosophy is merely about lionizing envy.) Some of that envy and resentment is a vice. But when the rich flaunt their exclusivity and engage in status-enhancing consumption, perhaps a little resentment and disgust is deserved.

Regarding the second worry: Back in 1930, the economist John Maynard Keynes wrote a remarkable essay called "Economic Possibilities for Our Grandchildren." He hypothesized that in one hundred years—by 2030—people in the UK would be eight times richer than they are in 1930, and that people around the world would in general be much richer. His predictions are on track to be correct. He also thought that eventually, if not necessarily by 2030, this would mean the economic problem would essentially be solved. Perhaps people would stop worrying about wealth and income per se, and instead get on with the art of living. He thought we might eventually come to have a shift in values, to caring less about work and thrift, and more about art and transcendent values.

He thought that it's OK to love money as of 1930, but maybe by 2130 we'd be so rich that it would make sense to detest it:

> There are changes in other spheres too which we must expect to come. When the accumulation of wealth is no longer of high social importance, there will be great changes in the code of morals. We shall be able to rid ourselves of many of the pseudo-moral principles which have hag-ridden us for two hundred years, by which we have exalted some of the most distasteful of human qualities into the position of the highest virtues. We shall be able to afford to dare to assess the money-motive at its true value. The love of money as a possession—as distinguished from the love of money as a means to the enjoyments and realities of life—will be recognised for what it is, a somewhat disgusting morbidity, one of those semicriminal, semi-pathological propensities which one hands over with a shudder to the specialists in mental disease. All kinds of social customs and economic practices, affecting the distribution of wealth and of economic rewards and penalties, which we now maintain at all costs, however distasteful and unjust they may be in themselves, because they are tremendously useful in promoting the accumulation of capital, we shall then be free, at last, to discard.[1]

Is Keynes right? Is there a certain point where it makes sense to stop caring about making more money? Should we—as so many 19th century classical economists thought—at some point have a stationary economy, an economy which simply maintains the current level of income with no further growth?

Let's jump back to examine automobile trends in 2014.

Back then, a Toyota Corolla LE—one of the most popular sedans in the United States—sold for about $20,000. *Motor Trend* estimates that the car's 1.8-liter four-banger and CVT manages 0–60 mph in a lethargic 9 seconds.[2] The interior materials are not cheap, per se, but the car is awash in boring cloth and hard plastic. The car handles about as well as a loaded shopping cart.

A properly outfitted BMW 328i—a common entry-level luxury sports sedan for working professionals—sold for about $49,000. Its turbo-charged, four-cylinder engine propels drivers from 0–60 in about 5.5 seconds, and the interior is finished in leather and soft materials. The car loves to corner.

The Hyundai Genesis—Hyundai's entry into the sports sedan market—offered similar performance and luxury to the 328i, but for less money. A fully loaded Genesis sold for about $44,000.

Still, the BMW 328i far outsold the Genesis, despite costing significantly more.[3] A significant reason why is that the BMW badge conveys far more prestige than the Hyundai. Hyundai itself acknowledged this. Older versions of the Genesis had only small or suppressed Hyundai logos. In 2018, as I write the first draft of this sentence, Hyundai has relaunched Genesis as a separate brand, moving toward separate dealerships, just as Audi is independent of Volkswagen and Lexus of Toyota.

The upshot: When one buys a BMW, one isn't just buying a car. One is buying status and an image.

Consider: Imagine a person had two cars available to him. The first is a regular BMW 328i. The second is also a BMW 328i, but has been modified to remove the BMW badges, kidney grille, and other identifying features. A typical person would be willing to pay much more for the first car over the second.

Similar remarks apply to watches. A Movado beats a Citizen, but an Oris beats a Movado, and a Patek Philippe beats an Oris. Still, at some point, the watches aren't really all that fancier, more attractive, or better made. At some point, the main thing one is paying for is the name. Perhaps the point of buying a Patek Philippe is to look down on people with Rolexes.

Some of these items may be what economists call "Veblen goods" (after economist Thorstein Veblen). With most goods, as the price decreases, the quantity demanded increases. For instance, Americans purchased almost 300,000 Toyota Corollas in 2012, but if Toyota managed to cut the price in half without sacrificing quality, they would sell far more. However, if BMW cut the price of the 328i to the price of a Toyota Corolla, it's possible BMW would then sell *fewer* cars.

The BMW 3 series may be a Veblen good. The point of buying a BMW is to be a member of a somewhat exclusive club. If the car becomes inexpensive, then buying the car no longer carries this perk. When you buy a BMW, you aren't just buying a performance-oriented luxury car. You are paying to express that you are more successful than other people. Similar remarks apply to Mercedes-Benz. It's thus no surprise that many BMW owners object to BMW introducing the relatively inexpensive 320i, while Mercedes-Benz fans are upset that Mercedes is introducing the relatively inexpensive CLA 250. Lowering the low end admits more people into the club and so reduces the exclusivity of the brand. The point of having a BMW or a Mercedes is, in part, to be the kind of person who has a BMW or a Mercedes. But that works only to the extent that most people can't afford a BMW or a Mercedes.

That's the psychology behind many luxury goods in a nutshell. Is it bad?

IS STATUS-SEEKING INHERENTLY REPUGNANT?

Human beings seem to be natural status-seekers. The ways in which status-seeking manifests may vary from culture to culture, but there seem to be no human cultures in which people do not seek status.

There's a clear problem with status-seeking: status-seeking is in the first instance a zero-sum game. We can all get smarter, but we can't all achieve the goal of being smarter than everyone else. We can all get richer, but we can't all be richer than everyone else. We can all become prettier, but we can't all be prettier than everyone else. Status is about ranking.

The only way to move up in the rankings is for someone else to move down. Consider: If we were to wave a magic wand that made all colleges in the United States twice as good as they are now, the US News and World Report college rankings should remain unchanged. If we were to wave a magic wand that made everyone twice as fast, it shouldn't change the outcome of the Olympic 100-meter race.

Because status is zero-sum, there is something intrinsically repugnant about status-seeking. To desire higher status is to desire superiority. To desire to increase one's rank is to desire that others' decrease their rank. But, ideally, social relationships would be positive sum-games, in which everyone can be a winner.

IS STATUS-SEEKING INSTRUMENTALLY USEFUL?

Ideally, I agree, everyone would overcome their thirst to be better than others. Ideally, everyone would work productively, innovate, and serve the common good out of public spirit, benevolence, and a desire to be excellent on absolute rather than on relative terms.[4] But, unfortunately, people are status-seekers. They seek status goods through markets and also outside of markets. Ironically, complaining about status-seeking is itself often a status-seeking activity: it's a thing we do to express our moral superiority.

Given that people are status-seeking, we might try to reduce this behavior. I don't see much hope for that. Thus, we should ask whether there is some way to transform the omnipresent zero-sum game of status-seeking into a positive-sum game.

Bernard Mandeville, in his famous poem "The Grumbling Hive," argued that markets have a tendency to do just that. He asks us to imagine a hive full of selfish bees, each trying to make a buck by supplying others' "lust and vanity." Yet while, "every Part" of this capitalist system is "full of Vice," the "whole Mass [is] a Paradise."[5] Even "the very Poor Lived better than the Rich before."[6] Mandeville's basic idea is that the inherently repugnant pursuit of status leads to innovation and economic growth in the long term. Status-seeking is gross, but markets can at least cause status-seeking to have a humanitarian pay-off.

The economist F. A. Hayek argues,

> Our rapid economic advancement is in large part a result of inequality and is impossible without it. Progress at a fast rate cannot proceed on a uniform front, but must take place in an echelon fashion. . . . At any stage of [the process of growing knowledge] there will always be many things we already know how to produce but which are still too expensive to provide for more than the few. . . . All of the conveniences of a comfortable home, of our means

of transportation, and communication, of entertainment and enjoyment, we could produce at first only in limited quantities; but it was in doing this that we gradually learned to make them or similar things at a much smaller outlay of resources and thus began to supply them to the great majority. A large part of the expenditure of the rich, though not intended for that end, thus serves to defray experimentation with the new things that, as a result, can later be made available to the poor.[7]

Hayek would say that the reason we're richer now than we were in the past is of course not because we have more resources—if anything, we have fewer. Instead, it's because we are more knowledgeable about how best to employ existing resources. But, typically, when we learn how to make something new, such as a cellular phone, it is very expensive to produce it on a per-unit basis. The rich buy the first units, get all of the benefits at first, but then also pay all of the up-front costs. They thereby pay for the basic infrastructure that makes it available for all. The rich pay for experimentation and innovation and fund entrepreneurs in finding ways to market to the poor, though this is not the intention of the rich. The reason wealthy countries today can provide what used to be luxuries (TVs, electricity, flush toilets) for all is because in the past those countries allowed such goods to be provided for just a few, rather than prohibited because not all can have them.

Allowing people to purchase status through markets has a unique feature—it generally causes status goods to become standard goods available to everyone. According to the US Census, more than 80.9% of US households below the poverty line have cell phones, 58.2% have computers, 83% have air conditioning, 68.7% have a clothes washer, 65.3% have a clothes dryer, and nearly 100% have refrigerators, stoves, and televisions.[8] When most of these items first appeared, only the rich could afford them. The rich buy them in part to have something no one else can afford. But in choosing to purchase such goods, the rich pay for the initial development of these goods, and in turn pay to make those goods available to a wider market. Those who want to buy status must then buy ever newer and fancier things, and the cycle repeats.

Lexus buyers pay Toyota to develop new and better engines and technology, which Toyota later inserts in its standard automobiles. Acura buyers do the same for Honda, Infiniti buyers the same for Nissan, and Cadillac buyers the same for GM. Today's premium becomes tomorrow's standard.

Consider the inexpensive Honda Fit, perhaps the best over-all car in the economy subcompact class. The car has a low-speed active braking system (the car will brake on its own to avoid accidents), paddle-shifters, ten beverage holders, two glove compartments, steering wheel-mounted controls, satellite navigation with voice controls, a USB audio interface, a six-speaker 160-Watt stereo system that plays mp3s and CDs, a touchscreen, traction control, forward and curtain airbags, anti-lock braking with electronic brake distribution, a smart drive-by-wire throttle system that manages the throttle in light of road and weather conditions, all while accelerating from a dead stop to 60 mph faster than a 1980s BMW, all while getting excellent fuel economy. Every feature—except the fuel economy—was originally available only at high cost to luxury car buyers.

So, again, I agree the desire to flaunt one's superiority to others is repugnant. But we should acknowledge it has some serious upsides.

ON THE WHOLE IDEA OF BUYING IMAGE

Buying the image *better than others* is repugnant, but as we saw, it at least has some hidden upsides. Some moralists go further, though, and say that buying image, period, is bad.

Activist-author Naomi Klein's book *No Logo* is a sustained attack on branding and brand identity. According to Klein, brand names originally developed during the industrial revolution as a way of differentiating similar products from one another. Brands can serve a legitimate function by helping us identify the products we prefer. So, for instance, we may genuinely prefer the taste of Coke to Pepsi, and branding allows us both to distinguish Coke from its competitors, and (in a regime where trademarks are respected) to distinguish authentic Coke from fake Coke.

Klein complains that brands have gone beyond their original legitimate mission. Branding is no longer about the product, but about the consumer of the product. In order to sell products, marketers construct and induce the public to accept certain connections between the products and lifestyles, images, and culture. So, for instance, Apple has managed to induce people to believe that Macs are cool—they are for exciting, creative, entrepreneurial, and artistic people—while PCs are boring—they are for accountants and fat gaming geeks. But, really, none of this has anything to do with the actual computers. Apple computers are not inherently more creative than PCs.

Corporations spend vast sums of money to manipulate us into accepting these product–lifestyle and product–image associations. LL Bean clothes are "outdoorsy" while equally rugged clothes by another manufacturer are "hip" and "streetwise." Marlboro cigarettes are rugged and manly, while otherwise identical cigarettes from a different manufacturer might be seen as wimpy or feminine. In the US, MLS soccer is seen as left wing, while NFL football is right wing. The Mazda 3 is cool and trendy, but other equally well-performing cars in its class are tedious and vanilla. Powerful Yogurt is for tough dudes, but otherwise identical Yoplait is for yoga chicks. Dos Equis beer is for interesting and exciting people, while Corona is for relaxing, while a case of Natty Light is the best beer for bros.

From a marketing perspective, the point of creating product–lifestyle and product–image association is to make it so that one's product is no longer a commodity. It allows the corporations to compete without necessarily having to make their products better. The Hyundai Genesis may be a better car than many other entry-level luxury cars, but it has difficulty competing because it lacks the right image. Constructing an image or culture around a product creates a barrier for entry into the market and helps keep a product's market share secure.

As far as I can tell, Klein doesn't have an explicit argument against branding so described. Rather, her main argument is rhetorical—she writes with a sense of dread, and uses conspiratorial imagery to induce a sense of alienation in the reader. Other than that, her main worries seem to be that such advertising is manipulative—marketers are, with the complicity of consumers, constructing a mythology about products out of thin air—and in some cases deceptive—marketers present the idea that buying products will transform a person from low to high status.

Contra Klein, I suspect that people *like* having product–lifestyle and product–image associations. Consider three possible worlds:

A. A world exactly like ours, with the extant product–lifestyle and product–image associations.

B. A world like ours, but with a different set of product–lifestyle and product–image associations of your choosing.

C. A world like ours, but with no product–lifestyle and product–image associations.

A is the status quo. B allows for the associations Klein dislikes, but has different associations. In B, you can decide that PCs are seen as artsy while Macs are seen as boring. In C, there are no associations at all. Products' reputations are entirely dependent upon the intrinsic qualities of those products, nothing more. Now ask: How would you rank A, B, and C?

I haven't conducted a poll, so I don't know what people would in fact choose. But I can make a case for choosing A and B over C. People have reason to value at least *some* product–lifestyle and product–image associations, if not all of them. My argument goes as follows:

1. The typical person desires to craft her identity, and desires to be able to express that identity to herself and to others.

2. When products have lifestyle, image, and cultural associations, the typical person can then use these products to help craft her identity, and to express that identity to herself and to others.

3. If so, then product–lifestyle and product–image associations are instrumentally valuable to the typical person.

4. Therefore, product–lifestyle and product–image associations are instrumentally valuable to the typical person.

I suspect premise 1 will seem obvious to anyone who has been a teenager or experienced the recent college graduate's "quarter-life crisis." In our culture, most of us at different points are faced with having to choose to create and cultivate a conception of the self. We choose among different sets of values and different ideas of what we should be. We don't simply *discover* ourselves, but actually choose who we will be.[9] We want to be able to express that identity to others, because we want them to see us in a certain light. We find it jarring for others to see us different from how we see ourselves or to fail to see us at all. We also want to express that identity to ourselves—which is why, for instance, some people still dress the same when no one is looking.

Regarding premise 2: When marketers, public relations experts, and brand-image consultants do their work—which requires cooperation from the public at large—they end up creating a rich palate of images, meanings, and ideas. I don't want to be overly precious about this, but in a sense, branding creates a richer set of colors by which we can paint our self-images, or it creates a richer set of materials by which we can construct our self-images. Just as poets and novelists draw upon preexisting imagery and allude to previous stories to express ideas, so we can do so, in much more mundane way, using brand imagery and brand mythology.

Now, it's possible that for any given person, or even for most people, the extant product–image and product–lifestyle associations are on the whole more oppressive than liberating. I haven't found an argument showing this is the case, but I'm open to the possibility. Yet even if someone did show that this were so, that would just demonstrate that for many people, C is preferable to A. It would not be a full defense of C, because one would still need to argue C is preferable to B.

NEVER ENOUGH

The World Bank estimated purchasing price parity-adjusted gross world product to be about $127.5 trillion in 2017. Suppose the economy *slows down* to a modest 2.5% per year for the next 50 years. Even on this pessimistic assumption—in fact, world product has been growing over 3.5%—gross world product will be over $430 trillion by 2068. By 2095, the average person alive should be as rich as the average Canadian or German right now.

Keynes wrote economics papers by day, but spent his nights reading poetry with other posh intellectuals in the Bloomsbury Group. He wondered if perhaps one day we'd all be like that— past the point of worrying so much about work and productivity, and instead concerned with higher things. Keynes thought we would encounter a new moral and intellectual crisis:

> for the first time since his creation man will be faced with his real, his permanent problem—how to use his freedom from pressing economic cares, how to occupy the leisure, which science and compound interest will have won for him, to live wisely and agreeably and well.[10]

Keynes has a point. In fact, as we discussed, people work fewer hours now than in the past and spend far more time on leisure. For some, leisure means pursuing a meaningful and productive hobby, such as knitting, gardening, playing an instrument, or discussing great literature. For others, leisure is largely about passive consumption—watching a football game or binging on Netflix. For some, it's a mix.

As Keynes predicted, our increased wealth has caused something of a moral and intellectual crisis. Some are perfectly happy to spend their lives in passive leisure, and some continue to feel that they must actively do something or their lives will lack meaning. Young adults are more likely now than in the past to face a "quarter-life crisis"—where they feel existential angst over having to decide what kind of person they will become. People recognize that choosing where to live and work is also choosing who they will be, what they will value, and whom they will come to love. Today, many people remain torn between incompatible lifestyles, for example, wanting to be a full-time mom and also have a full-time meaningful business career.[11]

Keynes speculated we'd eventually get rich enough that we'd conclude that we have enough "stuff." We would as a result develop new values and virtues designed to help us live meaningful lives. We would aim at artistic and intellectual endeavors rather than economic production per se. He thought we'd eventually come to see the old virtues of productivity and thrift as base—as virtues useful when we faced the economic problem of high scarcity but as repulsive once that problem was overcome.

Like Keynes, I am optimistic in the long run about humanity's ability to handle the "problems" created by abundance. I expect people's attitudes toward work and leisure to change as they enter an age of abundance, just as our own attitudes have already changed. For instance, 100 years ago, the typical American wasn't worried about finding "meaning" or fulfillment in their job.

Unlike Keynes, I am not enthusiastic about the prospect of a steady-state economy, that is, an economy that doesn't grow. I think there will always be a point to having more. I don't think there is ever "enough." I'll offer two reasons why, one negative and one positive.

The negative reason: A steady-state economy is by definition a zero-sum economy. If there is no economic growth, the only way one person can get richer is if another person becomes poorer. Consider a simple illustration. Suppose there are two people, Ann and Barbie. Suppose the total GDP of this two-person economy remains $1 million/year forever. In order for Ann to go from $500,000 to $600,000 of income, Barbie must go from $500,000 to $400,000. That's just a logical implication of a steady state.

I don't mean to exaggerate this point. When the typical philosopher talks of a steady-state economy, she normally doesn't mean to say we should force the system to remain zero-growth, to the point where we all become each other's economic adversaries. They just envision a system where most people are satisfied with what they have and there isn't much growth.

But, realistically, it seems that when there is low growth, people develop antipathy and antagonism toward one another.[12] They feel hopeless and unsatisfied. Perhaps in 200 years, we won't think this way anymore. But perhaps it's built into our psyches that we want our children to do better than we did. We don't really know.

The positive reason: I am optimistic about people's ability—in the long run—to do meaningful and amazing things when they have greater wealth. I expect that people will experiment with new forms of art and new ways of living. Some of those experiments will be successes, and people will transform the way they live and the way they extract meaning from life. I think there are higher forms of living and art we don't yet understand or imagine, but which require growth to achieve.

To give what might seem like a pedestrian or lowbrow example, consider video games. Note that I am hardly a gamer—I play and complete maybe one video game a decade. Nevertheless, I agree that some video games qualify as genuine works of art. For instance, consider Nintendo's *Legend of Zelda: The Breath of the Wild*. This game puts players in an immersive, gigantic open world, where they are free to complete a quest—or not—as they see fit, with complete freedom. The game encourages experimentation and entrepreneurship. Every puzzle can be solved a dozen ways—or ignored. It is also a profound—and often deeply moving—reflection on guilt, fear, failure, struggle, responsibility, loneliness, love, and redemption. Because the player actively controls a character rather than passively submits to a story, this art form allows people to experience emotions and release in a way that novels, films, musicals, or plays cannot. Now I'd love to see what the game developers could have done if they could have spent, say, $5 trillion creating this piece of art, rather than $100 million.[13]

The Marxist philosopher G. A. Cohen claimed that money— or rather the real wealth that money represents—is a form of freedom. The more one has, the more one can do. Wealth is a ticket to the world. It is more than that—it is the capacity to build and explore new worlds. If you share, as I do, a fundamental faith in humanity's long-term ability to find and develop new and better ways of living, then you would want our descendants to have as much of this kind of freedom as possible. In the long run, our descendants might live as gods, or rather as what we now imagine gods to be. I want to give them that chance.

CONCLUSION

Philosopher Thomas Hobbes famously said that people have a "perpetual desire for power after power, that ceaseth only in death."[14]

When most people hear or read this out of context— which is the way most people hear or read it—they assume that Hobbes has a pessimistic view of human nature, and that he means everyone wants to have power and domination *over* others.

Not so. Rather, Hobbes defines "power" as the capacity or means to obtain some future good. What Hobbes means by "perpetual desire for power after power" is that people have a constant desire to expand their capacity to obtain the good. Further, he thinks this motive is fully rational. After all, he says, even a person of moderate power is still under the threat of losing her means of living well or living at all. It makes sense to want more, because the more we have, the less vulnerable we are.

To be rich is to have power in this Hobbesian sense. Riches generally increase our capacity to achieve our ends. They insulate us from harm and risk. They expand our ability to lead lives that are authentically ours and to experience whatever joys the world can offer. They enable strangers to cooperate on the scale of billions and encourage us to put aside our differences.

THE ROOT OF ALL EVILS

1 Yes, that's a thing. I found dozens of examples, from $15–$30, on Google Shopping.
2 https://poetsandquants.com/2018/08/11/what-business-school-professors-are-paid-may-surprise-you/2/
3 www.independent.co.uk/life-style/british-sex-survey-2014-over-three-quarters-of-men-watch-porn-but-women-prefer-erotica-9762906.html
4 www.pewforum.org/religious-landscape-study/
5 Matthew 19:23–24.
6 http://historymatters.gmu.edu/d/5769/
7 In the King James edition, 1 Timothy 3:3, 1 Timothy 3:8, Titus 1:7, and 1 Peter 5:2.
8 www.ecnmy.org/engage/this-is-how-buddhist-monks-live-without-money/
9 Rousseau 1985.
10 Rathbone 2015.
11 Schopenhauer 2004.
12 www.law.com/almID/900005560787/?slreturn=20180929084833
13 www.cnbc.com/2017/06/06/bernie-sanders-made-over-1-million-last-year-and-has-joined-the-1-percent.html
14 Seneca, *Moral Letters to Lucilius*, letter 5. https://en.wikisource.org/wiki/Moral_letters_to_Lucilius/Letter_5
15 Isaacson 2009.
16 https://blogs.scientificamerican.com/moral-universe/the-problem-with-rich-people-and-ethics/
17 Cikara and Fiske 2012.
18 Durante, Tablante, and Fiske 2017; Liu, Zhang, and Hao 2017.
19 Piff et al. 2012.
20 Ariely and Mann 2013.
21 Bhattacharjee, Dana, and Baron 2017.
22 This is a terrible assumption. See William MacAskill 2015.
23 Sandel 2012.

24 Archard 1999.

25 Anderson 2000a.

26 Mitchell and Mickel 1999.

27 Bloch and Parry 1989.

28 See Brennan and Jaworski 2015.

29 Tetlock 2000.

30 For a review, see Brennan and Jaworski 2016.

31 McCloskey 2011 argues that changing attitudes towards money-making were essential in creating the great explosion of wealth in the West that began around the 1600s.

32 Maddison 2003, 70; The Maddison-Project, www.ggdc.net/maddison/maddison-project/home.htm, 2013 version.

33 From $130 constant 2000 US dollars in 5000 BC to $250 constant 2000 US dollars in 1800 AD according to Delong 2002, 120. Angus Maddison gives different numbers: $467 world GDP/capita in 1990 dollars in 1 AD up to $6516 world GDP/capita in 2003 AD, according to Maddison 2003, 70.

34 World per capita income as of 2014 is approximately $16,100 in 2014 US dollars, up from under $500 in 1800. www.cia.gov/library/publications/the-world-factbook/fields/2004.html

35 I use Angus Maddison's historical gdp/capita data, www.ggdc.net/maddison/Maddison.htm; plus World Bank data, https://data.worldbank.org/indicator/NY.GDP.MKTP.CD

36 I use Angus Maddison's historical gdp/capita data, www.ggdc.net/maddison/Maddison.htm. See also Maddison 2003.

37 Paul Krugman, "The CPI and the Rat Race," Slate, Sunday, December 22, 1996, www.slate.com/articles/business/the_dismal_science/1996/12/the_cpi_and_the_rat_race.html.

38 Sacerdote 2019.

39 U.S. Census Bureau, "American Housing Survey for the United States, 2003 and 2005 Data Charts," www.census.gov/hhes/www/housing/ahs/nationaldatahtml#jump2; U.S. Department of Energy, Energy Information Administration, "Housing Characteristics 2001," www.eia.doe.gov/emeu/recs/recs2001/detail_tables.html; U.S. Census Bureau, "Survey of Income and Program Participation," 2001 Panel, Wave 8 Topic Module, 2003.

40 Numbers derived from data at the US Census Bureau, "Annual Housing Survey," 2017, www.census.gov/programs-surveys/ahs/data/interactive/ahstablecreator.html

41 www.eia.gov/consumption/residential/data/2015/#electronics, Table HC4.5 Electronics in U.S. homes by household income, 2015.

42 US Census Bureau, "Survey of Income and Program Participation," 2001 Panel, Wave 8 Topical Module, 2003.

43 Nord et al. 2010, i, 10, 12.

44 Milanovic 2007.

45 Globalrichlist.org, using Milanovic 2007 data.

FOR THE LOVE OF MONEY

1 www.theguardian.com/news/datablog/2012/may/24/robert-kennedy-gdp

2 When somebody says, "GDP isn't all that matters, so you should give me more power!", it's naïve to think they're really interested in criticizing GDP.

3 Whillans et al. 2017.

4 Thanks to Chris Freiman for this point.

5 This paragraph paraphrases Schmidtz and Brennan 2010, 208.

6 E.g., see Diener, Lucas, and Scollon 2009; Mancini, Bonanno, and Clark 2011; Mochon, Norton, and Ariely 2008; Wu 2001; Frederick and Loewenstein 1999; Lyubomirsky 2010.

7 Easterlin 1974, 1995.

8 Stevenson and Wolfers 2008.

9 Kahneman 2006.

10 www.econlib.org/archives/2014/02/wolfers_respond.html

11 Stevenson and Wolfers 2008.

12 www.econlib.org/archives/2014/03/the_happiness_o.html

13 Cowen 2018, 42–43.

14 Berlin 1997, 177.

15 Cohen 1995, 58–59.

16 Hariri 2015, 79.

17 www.ggdc.net/maddison

18 www.globalrichlist.com

19 www.aei.org/publication/how-are-we-doing/

20 www.aei.org/publication/how-are-we-doing/

21 McCloskey 2006, 18–20.

22 https://ourworldindata.org/child-mortality

23 Easterbrook 2004, xiv.

24 Clark 2008, 249–252.

25 Pinker 2002, 57.

26 Pinker 2002, 57.

27 https://ourworldindata.org/war-and-peace

28 www.emdat.be/disaster_trends/index.html

29 See van der Vossen and Brennan 2018; https://ourworldindata.org/natural-catastrophes

30 www.aei.org/publication/how-are-we-doing/

31 Nordhaus 2010.
32 United Nations 2015, 1.
33 Stern 2007.
34 McCloskey 2006, 20.
35 Cowen 2002.
36 Finkel 2017.
37 www.nytimes.com/2014/02/15/opinion/sunday/the-all-or-nothing-marriage.html?_r=0
38 https://economix.blogs.nytimes.com/2012/02/06/marriage-is-for-rich-people/
39 Store managers can decide by fiat on the sticker price of a good, but they cannot usually decide by fiat what the good will actually sell for. If they set the price too high, people won't buy it, and if they set it too low, it will fly off the shelves and be resold at a higher price in the secondary market.
40 In the language of economics, in this scenario, there has been both a supply and a demand shock. There is a supply shock, because the lack of power makes it harder to produce ice or prevent the current stock from melting. There is a demand shock, because the power outage means that more people need ice and are willing to pay more for it.

IS MONEY DIRTY? DOES MONEY CORRUPT?

1 Levitt and Dubner 2008, 15–16.
2 Sandel 2012, 64–65; Satz 2010, 193–194.
3 Henrich et al. 2001.
4 www.bostonreview.net/gintis-giving-economists-their-due
5 See Brennan and Jaworski 2016.
6 Francois and Van Ypersele 2009.
7 Ariely et al. 2014.
8 Zak and Knack 2001.
9 Al-Ubayli et al. 2013.
10 Hoffman and Morgan 2015.
11 www.bbc.co.uk/news/science-environment-23623157
12 Camera, Casari, and Bigon 2013.
13 Lacetera, Macis, and Slonim 2013.
14 Jaworsi and English 2019.
15 Cameron and Pierce 1994.
16 Mitchell and Mickel 1999, 569.
17 Bloch and Parry 1989, 9.
18 Zelizer 1994, 2007, 2013.
19 Bloch and Parry 1989, 9.
20 Bloch and Parry 1989, 19–33.

21 Zelizer 1994.

22 von Neumann and Morgenstern 1944.

IT'S OK TO MAKE MONEY

1 http://fortune.com/2015/09/14/pope-francis-capitalism-inequality/

2 For a good review, see Renwick Monroe 2017; Renwick Monroe, Martin, and Ghosh 2009.

3 See Boom 2013.

4 www.scientificamerican.com/article/the-moral-life-of-babies/

5 Keynes 1930.

6 See MacAskill 2015.

7 More precisely, they ensure that for you to make a trade from which you expect to profit, the other parties also have to expect to profit. Sometimes we make mistakes. I've bought candy bars, expecting them to be worth more than the money I paid, only to discover I don't like that kind of candy. But at least we learn from experience and do better next time. And at least, going in, everyone reasonably expects to be made better off.

8 Cohen 2008.

9 Ricardo 1817, c2, §§2.3–2.5.

10 www.scribd.com/document/166175880/Reason-Rupe-Poll-May-2013-Toplines

11 http://pages.stern.nyu.edu/~adamodar/New_Home_Page/datafile/margin.html

12 www.macrotrends.net/stocks/charts/WMT/walmart/net-profit-margin

13 Schmidtz and Brennan 2010, 198.

14 McCloskey 1992, 112.

15 Smith 1776, 145.

16 For a review, see Svorny 2004.

17 https://ij.org/issues/economic-liberty/braiding/

18 https://ij.org/case/taalib-din-abdul-uqdah-v-district-of-columbia-2/

19 https://wol.iza.org/uploads/articles/392/pdfs/the-influence-of-occupational-licensing-and-regulation.pdf

20 www.forbes.com/sites/stevensalzberg/2016/04/25/why-are-we-growing-corn-to-fuel-our-cars-three-reasons-why-ethanol-is-a-bad-idea/#6d971ff95e98; http://science.sciencemag.org/content/319/5867/1238

21 www.npr.org/sections/itsallpolitics/2013/11/11/243973620/when-lobbyists-literally-write-the-bill; www.theatlantic.com/business/archive/2015/04/how-corporate-lobbyists-conquered-american-democracy/390822/

22 www.cato.org/publications/commentary/why-enron-wants-global-warming

RICH COUNTRY, POOR COUNTRY

1 One might object that whether one has good or bad institutions today depends upon whether one was colonized in the past. Acemoglu, Johnson, and Robinson 2005 instead show that the issue is more complicated. Some colonized countries are richer today than they otherwise would have been because the colonizing powers installed good institutions. (This is not meant to excuse or defend colonization.) Some are poorer because the colonizing powers instead installed extractive institutions.

2 Acemoglu, Johnson, and Robinson 2005; Acemoglu and Robinson 2013; Cowen and Tabarrok 2010, 92–106; North 1990; North, Wallis, and Weingast 2012; Rodrik, Subramanian, and Trebbi 2004.

3 North 1990, 3.

4 Roland 2014, 108.

5 Rodrik, Subramanian, and Trebbi 2004, 13; Risse 2005 Similarly, Cowen and Tabarrok 2010, 101, summarize, "the key to producing and organizing the factors of production [in ways that lead to prosperity] are institutions that create appropriate incentives."

6 Beckert 2015; Johnson 2013; Baptist 2016 See Olmstead and Rhode 2018 for a damning critique. See also http://bradleyahansen.blogspot.com/2014/10/the-back-of-ed-baptists-envelope.html

7 www.salon.com/2014/09/07/we_still_lie_about_slavery_heres_the_truth_about_how_the_american_economy_and_power_were_built_on_forced_migration_and_torture/

8 Maddison-Project, www.ggdc.net/maddison/maddison-project/home.htm, 2013 version; Landes 1999, xx.

9 As economist Angus Maddison summarizes the trends (Maddison 2003, 70–71):

> In the year 1000 the inter-regional spread was very narrow indeed. By 2003 all regions had increased their incomes, but there was an 18:1 gap between the richest and poorest region, and a much wider inter-country spread.
>
> One can also see the divergence between the 'west' (western Europe, US, Canada, Australia, New Zealand) and the rest of the world economy. Real per capita income in the west increased 2.8-fold between the year 1000 and 1820, and 20-fold from 1820 to 2003. In the rest of the world income rose much more slowly—slightly more than a quarter from 1000 to 1820 and seven-fold since then.

10 http://data.worldbank.org/indicator/NY.GDP.PCAP.PP.CD

11 Maddison 2003, 70–71.

12 Chart made using data from Maddison 2003, 70.

13 Acemoglu and Robinson 2005, 2013; Acemoglu, Johnson, and Robinson 2001, 2002; Hall and Jones 1999; Hall and Lawson 2015; De Soto 2000.

14 Leeson 2010.

15 Leeson 2010.

16 Gwartney, Lawson, and Hall 2015, 2017.

17 Gwartney, Lawson, and Hall 2015, 24.

18 Rodrik, Subramanian, and Trebbi 2004 suggest that institutional quality is the main explanatory variable of growth. See also Acemoglu and Robinson 2005; Acemoglu, Johnson, and Robinson 2001, 2002; Hall and Jones 1999; Hall and Lawson 2014; De Soto 2000; Easterly and Ross 2003.

19 Acemoglu and Robinson 2013, 74–75.

20 Acemoglu and Robinson 2013, 372–373.

21 Pogge 2001, 65.

22 Weil 2013, 453.

23 Arezki, van der Ploeg, and Toscani 2019.

24 Weil 2013, 450.

25 Weil 2013, 450–451.

26 http://www2.ohchr.org/english/issues/poverty/expert/docs/Thomas_Pogge_Summary.pdf

27 Others have found similar results. For example, Robert Grier argues that the current economic performance of former colonies is strongly correlated with how long European powers held those colonies. See Grier 1999.

28 Smith 1776.

29 Smith 1776, V.3.92.

30 Smith 1776, IV.vii.c.17.

31 E.g., O'Brien 1988; Offer 1993; Davis and Huttenback 1982, 1987; Cunningham 1983; Edelstein 1982; Foreman-Peck 1989; Coelho 1973; McDonald 2009; Fieldhouse 1961.

32 Davis and Huttenback 1987 finds this is precisely what happened. The benefits of imperials were concentrated among the politically well-connected few.

33 https://en.wikipedia.org/wiki/1860_United_States_Census

34 www.measuringworth.com/slavery.php

35 Ransom and Sutch 1988.

36 Conrad and Meyer 1958; Carter et al. 2006; Sutch 1965; Murray et al. 2015; Stanley Lebergott 1981.

37 Whaples 1995.

38 Nunn 2008.

39 Wright 2006, 2017; Engerman and Sokoloff 1997, 2002; Sokoloff, Kenneth, and Engerman 2000; Meyer 1988, 2017.

40 Beckert 2014, xv, 95.

41 In a number of places, Olmstead and Rhode trace Baptist's quotations back to Baptist's sources. They find that Baptist inserts words, phrases, and entire sentences into some quotations, or drops words, sentences, and context from others, in order to alter their meaning to fit his narrative. Whether this was intentional academic fabrication or simple incompetence, only Baptist knows.

42 Olmstead and Rhode 2018, 1. See also Engerman 2017.

43 Olmstead and Rhode 2018.

44 Omstead and Rhode 2018.

45 Olmstead and Rhode 2018.

46 US Census 1861, 733–742, www.census.gov/programs-surveys/decen nial-census/decade/decennial-publications.1860.html;https://www2. census.gov/library/publications/decennial/1860/manufactures/ 1860c-22.pdf?#

47 Baptist 2016, 321–322.

48 http://bradleyahansen.blogspot.com/2014/10/the-back-of-ed-bap tists-envelope.html

49 http://bradleyahansen.blogspot.com/2014/10/the-back-of-ed-bap tists-envelope.html

50 Olmstead and Rhode 2018, 12.

51 https://georgetown.app.box.com/s/n6jizt11blybpeusicxq0kvmn7 go8cz6

52 www.ggdc.net/maddison/oriindex.htm

53 Thanks to Daniel Bier for this point. See Lebergott 1981, 883.

54 Thanks to Phil Magness for this point. See Surdam 1998.

55 Magness 2018.

GIVE IT AWAY NOW?

1 Schmidtz 2006, 92.

2 Frank 1984; Krugman and Wells 2012, 319–322, 552–554; Mankiw 2014, 260–262; Isen 2015.

3 Isen 2015; Frank 1984; Krugman and Wells 2012, 319–322, 552–554; Mankiw 2014, 260–262.

4 Isen 2015.

5 Schmidtz 2006, 91.

6 See Tosi and Warmke 2020; Simler and Hanson 2018.

7 www.youtube.com/watch?v=lC4FnfNKwUo

8 www.givingwhatwecan.org/research/other-causes/blindness/

9 Singer 1972, 231.

10 Singer 1972, 231.

11 Singer 1972, 232.

12 Singer 1972, 231.

13 www.businessinsider.com/the-worlds-best-charity-can-save-a-life-for-333706-and-thats-a-steal-2015-7

14 Singer 2010, 3.

15 www.princeton.edu/news/2018/10/08/princeton-endowment-earns-142-percent-return

16 Unger 1996, 20.

17 Schmidtz 2008, 157.

18 Schmidtz 2008, 157–158.

19 Deaton 2013, 268–269.

20 https://nccs.urban.org/data-statistics/charitable-giving-america-some-facts-and-figures

21 Coyne 2013, 47.

22 Deaton 2013, 285.

23 Doucouliagos and Paldam 2006, 2009; Elbadawi 1999; Lensink and White 2001.

24 Here, I draw from Coyne 2013, 51. See also Banerjee and Duflo 2011; Collier 2007; Easterly 2002, 2006; Moyo 2009; Hubbard and Duggan 2009; Karlan and Appel 2011. Some studies claim to find that aid often has a positive effective on growth, but only on the condition that the recipient country already has good institutions, such as strong protections of private property and the rule of law. (See Burnside and Dollar 2000.) These studies corroborate the "institutions trump everything else" story: aid is helpful only if the right institutions are in place. Other studies claim to find that aid always has *some* positive effect, even without good background institutions. (E.g., see Hansen and Tarp 2001.) But most other studies claim to find *no* effect, or, even worse, that aid has a negative effect (Brumm 2003; Rajan and Subramanian 2008; Bauer 2000; Easterly, Levine, and Roodman 2004; Doucouliagos and Paldam 2006, 2009; Elbadawi 1999; Lensink and White 2001).

25 Acemoglu and Robinson 2013, 452–453.

26 van der Vossen and Brennan 2018.

RICHES, REPUGNANCE, AND REMAINING DOUBTS

1 www.econ.yale.edu/smith/econ116a/keynes1.pdf

2 www.motortrend.com/roadtests/sedans/1306_2014_toyota_corolla_first_look/

3 www.goodcarbadcar.net/2011/01/hyundai-genesis-sales-figures/; www.goodcarbadcar.net/2011/01/bmw-3-series-sales-figures/

4 For an account of what markets would look like in such a world, see Jason Brennan, *Why Not Capitalism?* (New York: Routledge Press, 2014).

5 Mandeville 1988, 24.

6 Mandeville 1988, 26.

7 Hayek 1960, 42–44.
8 www.census.gov/hhes/well-being/publications/extended-11.html
9 For an account of how this might be done see Brennan 2005.
10 Keynes 1930.
11 Stevenson and Wolfers 2009.
12 Freidman 2006.
13 www.forbes.com/sites/olliebarder/2016/06/30/zelda-breath-of-the-
   wild-needs-to-sell-2-million-copies-to-break-even/#1ea4b68a615f
14 Hobbes 1994, XI.ii.

Bibliography

Acemoglu, Daron, Simon Johnson, and James A. Robinson. 2001. "The Colonial Origins of Comparative Development: An Empirical Investigation." *American Economic Review* 91: 1369–1401.

Acemoglu, Daron, Simon Johnson, and James A. Robinson. 2002. "Reversal of Fortune: Geography and Institutions in the Making of World Income Distribution." *Quarterly Journal of Economics* 117: 1231–1294.

Acemoglu, Daron, Simon Johnson, and James A. Robinson. 2005. "Institutions as a Fundamental Cause of Long-Run Growth." In *Handbook of Economic Growth*, Vol. 1A, edited by Philippe Aghion and Steven N. Darlauf. Amsterdam: Elsevier.

Acemoglu, Daron, and James A. Robinson. 2005. "Unbundling Institutions." *Journal of Political Economy* 113: 949–995.

Acemoglu, Daron, and James A. Robinson. 2013. *Why Nations Fails*. New York: Crown Business.

Al-Ubayli, Omar, Daniel Houser, John Nye, Maria Pia Paganelli, and Xiaofei Sophia Pan. 2013. "The Causal Effect of Market Priming on Trust: An Experimental Investigation Using Randomized Control." *PLoS One* 8 (3): e55968. doi:10.1371/journal.pone.0055968.

Anderson, Elizabeth. 2000a. "Why Commercial Surrogate Motherhood Unethically Commodifies Women and Children: Reply to McLachlan and Swales." *Health Care Analysis* 8: 19–26.

Anderson, Elizabeth. 2000b. "Beyond Homo Economicus: New Developments in Theories of Social Norms." *Philosophy and Public Affairs* 29: 170–200.

Archard, David. 1999. "Selling Yourself: Titmuss's Argument Against a Market in Blood." *Journal of Ethics* 6: 87–102.

Arezki, Rabah, Frederick van der Ploeg, and Frederik Toscani. 2019. "The Shifting Natural Wealth of Nations: The Role of Market Orientation." *Journal of Development Economics* 138: 228–245.

Ariely, Dan, Ximena Garcia-Rada, Lars Hornuf, and Heather Mann. 2014. "The (True) Legacy of Two Really Existing Economic Systems." Munich

Discussion Paper No. 2014-26. https://papers.ssrn.com/sol3/papers.cfm? abstract_id=2457000.

Ariely, Dan, and Heather Mann. 2013. "A Bird's Eye View of Unethical Behavior: Commentary on Trautmann et al." *Perspectives on Psychological Science* 8: 498–500.

Banerjee, Abhijit, and Esther Duflo. 2011. *Poor Economics*. New York: Public Affairs.

Baptist, Edward. 2016. *The Half Has Never Been Told*. New York: Basic Books.

Barber, Benjamin. 2008. *Consumed*. New York: W. W. Norton and Company.

Bauer, Peter T. 2000. *From Subsistence to Exchange*. Princeton: Princeton University Press.

Becker, Gary. 1957. *The Economics of Discrimination*. Chicago: University of Chicago Press.

Beckert, Sven. 2014. *Empire of Cotton*. New York: Penguin.

Beckert, Sven. 2015. *Empire of Cotton*. New York: Vintage.

Benhabib, Seyla. 2004. *The Rights of Others*. New York: Cambridge University Press.

Berggren, Niclas, and Therese Nilsson. 2013. "Does Economic Freedom Foster Tolerance?" *Kyklos* 66: 177–207.

Berlin, Isaiah. 1997. "Two Concepts of Liberty." In *The Proper Study of Mankind*. New York: Farrar, Straus, Giroux.

Bhattacharjee, Amit, Jason Dana, and Jonathan Baron. 2017. "Anti-Profit Beliefs: How People Neglect the Societal Benefits of Profit." *Journal of Personality and Social Psychology* 113: 671.

Bloch, Maurice, and Jonathan Parry. 1989. *Money and the Morality of Exchange*. New York: Cambridge University Press.

Boom, Paul. 2013. *Just Babies: The Origins of Good and Evil*. New York: Crown.

Boswell, Samuel. 2008. *The Life of Johnson*. New York: Penguin.

Brennan, Jason. 2005. "Choice and Excellence: A Defense of Millian Individualism." *Social Theory and Practice* 31: 483–498.

Brennan, Jason. 2014. *Why Not Capitalism?* New York: Routledge Press.

Brennan, Jason, and Peter Jaworski. 2015. "Markets Without Symbolic Limits." *Ethics* 125: 1053–1077.

Brennan, Jason, and Peter Jaworski. 2016. *Markets Without Limits*. New York: Routledge Press.

Brian, Craig, and Brian Lowery. 2009. *1001 Quotations That Connect: Timeless Wisdom for Preaching, Teaching, and Writing*. Grand Rapids: Zondervan Press.

Brumm, Harold J. 2003. "Aid, Policies, and Growth: Bauer Was Right." *Cato Journal* 23: 167–174.

Burnside, Craig, and David Dollar. 2000. "Aid, Policies, and Growth." *American Economic Review* 90: 847–868.

Camera, Gabriele, Marco Casari, and Maria Bigoni. 2013. "Money and Trust Among Strangers." *Proceedings of the National Academy of Sciences* 110: 14889–14893.

Cameron, Judy, and W. David Pierce. 1994. "Reinforcement, Reward, and Intrinsic Motivation: A Meta-Analysis." *Review of Educational Research* 64: 363–423.

Carter, Susan B., Scott Sigmund Gartner, Michael R. Haines, Alan L. Olmstead, Richard Sutch, and Gavin Wright, eds. 2006. *Historical Statistics of the United States: Earliest Times to the Present.* New York: Cambridge University Press.

Cikara, Mina, and Susan T. Fiske. 2012. "Stereotypes and Schadenfreude: Affective and Physiological Markers of Pleasure at Outgroup Misfortunes." *Social Psychological and Personality Science* 3: 63–71.

Clark, Gregory. 2008. *A Farewell to Alms.* Princeton: Princeton University Press.

Coelho, Philip R. P. 1973. "The Profitability of Imperialism: The British Experience in the West Indies." *Explorations in Economic History* 10: 253–280.

Cohen, G. A. 1995. *Self-Ownership, Freedom, and Equality.* New York: Cambridge University Press.

Cohen, G. A. 2008. *Why Not Socialism?* Princeton: Princeton University Press.

Collier, Paul. 2007. *The Bottom Billion: Why the Poorest Countries Are Failing and What Can Be Done About It.* New York: Oxford University Press.

Conrad, Alfred, and John Meyer. 1958. "The Economics of Slavery in the Antebellum South." *Journal of Political Economy* 66: 95–130.

Cowen, Tyler. 2002. *Creative Destruction.* Princeton: Princeton University Press.

Cowen, Tyler. 2018. *Stubborn Attachments.* San Francisco: Stripe Press.

Cowen, Tyler, and Alex Tabarrok. 2010. *Modern Principles of Economics.* New York: Worth.

Coyne, Christopher. 2013. *Doing Bad by Doing Good: Why Humanitarian Aid Fails.* Stanford: Stanford University Press.

Cunningham Wood, John. 1983. *British Economists and the Empire.* New York: St. Martin's Press.

Davis, Lance E., and Robert A. Huttenback. 1982. "The Political Economy of British Imperialism: Measures of Benefits and Support." *Journal of Economic History* 42: 119–130.

Davis, Lance E., and Robert A. Huttenback. 1987. *Mammon and Empire.* New York: Cambridge University Press.

De Soto, Hernando. 2000. *The Mystery of Capital.* New York: Basic Books.

Deaton, Angus. 2013. *The Great Escape.* Princeton: Princeton University Press.

Deci, E. L., R. Koestner, and R. M. Ryan. 1999. "A Meta-Analytic Review of Experiments Examining the Effects of Extrinsic Rewards on Intrinsic Motivation." *Psychological Bulletin* 125: 627–668.

Delong, Brad. 2002. *Macroeconomics.* New York: McGraw-Hill.

Diener, E., Richard E. Lucas, and Christie Napa Scollon. 2009. "Beyond the Hedonic Treadmill: Revising the Adaptation Theory of Well-Being." In *The Science of Well-Being*, 103–118. Dordrecht: Springer.

Doucouliagos, Hristos, and Martin Paldam. 2006. "Aid Effectiveness on Accumulation: A Meta Study." *Kyklos* 59: 227–254.

Doucouliagos, Hristos, and Martin Paldam. 2009. "The Aid Effectiveness Literature: The Sad Results of 40 Years of Research." *Journal of Economic Surveys* 23: 433–461.

Durante, Federica, Courney Beans Tablante, and Susan Fiske. 2017. "Poor but Warm, Rich but Cold (and Competent), Social Classes on the Stereotype Model." *Journal of Social Issues* 73: 138–157.

Easterbrook, Gregg. 2004. *The Progress Paradox*. New York: Random House.

Easterlin, Richard A. 1974. "Does Economic Growth Improve the Human Lot? Some Empirical Evidence." In *Nations and Households in Economic Growth*, edited by R. David and R. Reder, 89–125. New York: Academic Press.

Easterlin, Richard A. 1995. "Will Raising the Incomes of All Increase the Happiness of All?" *Journal of Economic Behavior & Organization* 27: 35–47.

Easterly, William. 2002. *The Elusive Quest for Growth*. Cambridge, MA: MIT Press.

Easterly, William. 2006. *The White Man's Burden*. Oxford University Press.

Easterly, William, Roberta Gatti, and Sergio Kurlat. 2006. "Development, Democracy, and Mass Killings." *Journal of Economic Growth* 11: 129–156.

Easterly, William, and Ross Levine. 2003. "Tropics, Germs, and Crops: How Endowments Influence Economic Development." *Journal of Monetary Economics* 50: 3–39.

Easterly, William, Ross Levine, and David Roodman. 2004. "Aid, Policies, and Growth: Comment." *American Economic Review* 94: 774–780.

Easterly, William, and Yaw Nyarko. 2009. "Is the Brain Drain Good for Africa?" In *Skilled Immigration Today: Prospects, Problems, and Policies*, edited by Jagdish Bhagwati and Gordon Hanson. Oxford University Press.

Edelstein, Michael. 1982. *Overseas Investment in the Age of High Imperialism: The United Kingdom, 1850–1914*. New York: Columbia University Press.

Eisenberger, Robert, and Judy Cameron. 1996. "Detrimental Effects of Reward: Reality or Myth?" *American Psychologist* 51: 1154–1166.

Elbadawi, I. A. 1999. "External Aid: Help or Hindrance to Export Orientation in Africa." *Journal of African Economics* 8: 578–616.

Engerman, Stanley L. 2017. "Review of *The Business of Slavery and the Rise of American Capitalism, 1815–1860* by Calvin Schermerhorn and *The Half Has Never Been Told* by Edward E. Baptist." *Journal of Economic Literature* 55: 637–643.

Engerman, Stanley L., and Kenneth L. Sokoloff. 1997. "Factor Endowments, Institutions, and Differential Paths of Growth Among New World

Why It's OK to Want to Be Rich

Economies." In *How Latin America Fell Behind*, 260–304. Stanford: Stanford University Press.

Engerman, Stanley L., and Kenneth L. Sokoloff. 2002. *Factor Endowments, Inequality, and Paths of Development Among New World Economics*. No. w9259. National Bureau of Economic Research.

Fabre, Cécile. 2006. *Whose Body Is It Anyway?* New York: Oxford University Press.

Fieldhouse, D. K. 1961. "'Imperialism': A Historiographical Revision." *Economic History Review* 14: 187–209.

Finkel, Eli. 2017. *The All or Nothing Marriage*. New York: Dutton.

Foreman-Peck, J. 1989. "Foreign Investment and Imperial Exploitation: Balance of Payments Reconstruction for Nineteenth-Century Britain and India." *Economic History Review* 42: 354–374.

Francois, P., and T. Van Ypersele. 2009. "Doux Commerces: Does Market Competition Cause Trust?" CEPR Discussion Paper No. DP7368.

Frank, Robert. 1984. "Are Workers Paid Their Marginal Products?" *American Economic Review* 74: 549–571.

Frederick, Shane, and George Loewenstein. 1999. "16 Hedonic Adaptation." In *Well-Being: The Foundations of Hedonic Psychology*, edited by D. Kahneman, E. Diener, and N. Schwarz, 302–329. New York: Russell Sage.

Freidman, Benjamin. 2006. *The Moral Consequences of Economic Growth*. New York: Vintage.

Gorman, Linda. 2013. "Discrimination." In *The Concise Encyclopedia of Economics*, 2013 online ed. www.econlib.org/library/Enc1/Discrimination.html.

Grier, Robert. 1999. "Colonial Legacies and Economic Growth." *Public Choice* 98: 317–335.

Gwartney, James, Robert Lawson, and Joshua Hall. 2015. *Economic Freedom of the World, 2014 Report*. Vancouver: Fraser Institute.

Gwartney, James, Robert Lawson, and Joshua Hall. 2017. *Economic Freedom of the World, 2016 Report*. Vancouver: Fraser Institute.

Hall, Joshua, and Robert A. Lawson. 2014. "Economic Freedom of the World: An Accounting of the Literature." *Contemporary Economic Policy* 32: 1–19.

Hall, Joshua, and Robert A. Lawson. 2015. "Economic Freedom of the World: An Accounting of the Literature." *Contemporary Economic Policy* 32: 1–19.

Hall, Robert, and Charles Jones. 1999. "Why Do Some Countries Produce so Much More Output per Worker than Others?" *Quarterly Journal of Economics* 114: 83–116.

Hansen, Henrik, and Finn Tarp. 2001. "Aid and Growth Regressions." *Journal of Development Economics* 64: 547–570.

Hariri, Yuval Noah. 2015. *Sapiens*. New York: Harper.

Hayek, F. A. 1960. *The Constitution of Liberty.* Chicago: University of Chicago Press.

Henrich, J., R. Boyd, S. Bowles, C. Camerer, E. Fehr, H. Gintis, and R. McElreath. 2001. "In Search of Homo Economicus: Behavioral Experiments in 15 Small-Scale Societies." *The American Economic Review* 91: 73–78.

Hobbes, Thomas. 1994. *Leviathan.* Indianapolis: Hackett.

Hoffman, Mitchell, and John Morgan. 2015. "Who's Naughty? Who's Nice? Experiments on Whether Pro-Social Workers Are Selected Out of Cutthroat Business Environments." *Journal of Economic Behavior & Organization* 109: 173–187.

Hubbard, R. Glenn, and William Duggan. 2009. *The Aid Trap: Hard Truths About Ending Poverty.* New York: Columbia Business School Publishing.

Isaacson, Walter. 2009. *Steve Jobs.* New York: Simon and Schuster.

Isen, Adam. 2015. "Dying to Know: Are Workers Paid Their Marginal Products?" Working Paper, Wharton School of Business.

Jaworsi, Peter, and William English. 2019. "Paid Plasma Has Not Decreased Unpaid Blood Donations." Working Paper.

Jha, Saumitra. 2013. "Trade, Institutions, and Ethnic Tolerance: Evidence from South Asia." *American Political Science Review* 107: 806–832.

Johnson, Walter. 2013. *River of Dark Dreams.* Cambridge, MA: Belknap Press.

Kahneman, Daniel. 2006. "The Sad Tale of the Aspirational Treadmill." In *The World Question Center*, edited by John Brockman. www.edge.org/q2008/q08_17.html#kahneman.

Karlan, Dean, and Jacob Appel. 2011. *More than Good Intentions: Improving the Ways the Poor Borrow, Save, Learn, and Stay Healthy.* New York: Plume.

Keynes, John Maynard. 1930. "Economic Possibilities for Our Grandchildren." www.econ.yale.edu/smith/econ116a/keynes1.pdf.

Krugman, Paul, and Robin Wells. 2012. *Microeconomics.* 3rd ed. New York: Worth Publishers.

Lacetera, N., M. Macis, and R. Slonim. 2013. "Economic Rewards to Motivate Blood Donations." *Science* 340: 927–928.

Landes, David. 1999. *The Wealth and Poverty of Nations: Why Some Are So Rich and Some Are So Poor.* New York: W. W. Norton and Co.

Lebergott, Stanley. 1981. "Thought the Blockade: The Profitability and Extent of Cotton Smuggling, 1861–1865." *The Journal of Economic History* 41: 867–888.

Leeson, Peter. 2010. "Two Cheers for Capitalism?" *Society* 47: 227–233.

Lensink, R., and H. White. 2001. "Are There Negative Returns to Aid?" *Journal of Development Studies* 37: 42–65.

Levitt, Steven, and Stephen Dubner. 2008. *Freakonomics.* New York: William Morrow.

Liu, Chang-Jiang, Yue Zhang, and Fang Hao. 2017. "An Implicit Stereotype of the Rich and Its Relation to Psychological Connectedness." *Journal of Pacific Rim Psychology* 11: e7.

Lyubomirsky, Sonja. 2010. "11 Hedonic Adaptation to Positive and Negative Experiences." In *The Oxford Handbook of Stress, Health, and Coping*, 200–224. New York: Oxford University Press.

MacAskill, William. 2015. *Doing Good Better*. New York: Avery.

Maddison, Angus. 2003. *Contours of the World Economy, 1–2030 AD: Essays in Macro-Economic History*. New York: Oxford University Press.

Magness, Philip. 2018. "Classical Liberalism and the 'New' History of Capitalism." In *What Is Classical Liberal History*, edited by Michael Douma and Phillip Magness, 17–38. Landham, MD: Lexington Books.

Mancini, Anthony D., George A. Bonanno, and Andrew E. Clark. 2011. "Stepping Off the Hedonic Treadmill." *Journal of Individual Differences* 32: 144–152.

Mandeville, Bernard. 1988. *The Fable of the Bees*. Indianapolis: Liberty Fund.

Mankiw, N. Gregory. 2014. *Principles of Economics*. 7th ed. New York: Cengage Learning.

McCloskey, Deirdre. 1992. *If You're so Smart*. Chicago: University of Chicago Press.

McCloskey, Deirdre. 2006. *The Bourgeois Virtues*. Chicago: University of Chicago Press.

McCloskey, Deirdre. 2011. *Bourgeois Dignity*. Chicago: University of Chicago Press.

McDonald, Paul. 2009. "Those Who Forget Historiography Are Doomed to Republish It: Empire, Imperialism, and Contemporary Debates About American Power." *Review of International Studies* 35: 45–67.

Meyer, David R. 1988. "The Industrial Retardation of Southern Cities, 1860–1880." *Explorations in Economic History* 25 (4): 366–386.

Meyer, John R. 2017. *The Economics of Slavery: And Other Studies in Econometric History*. Routledge.

Milanovic, Branko. 2007. *The Haves and the Have Nots*. New York: Basic Books.

Mitchell, Terence R., and Amy E. Mickel. 1999. "The Meaning of Money: An Individual-Difference Perspective." *Academy of Management Review* 24: 568–578.

Mochon, Daniel, Michael I. Norton, and Dan Ariely. 2008. "Getting Off the Hedonic Treadmill, One Step at a Time: The Impact of Regular Religious Practice and Exercise on Well-Being." *Journal of Economic Psychology* 29: 632–642.

Moyo, Dambiso. 2009. *Dead Aid: Why Aid Is Not Working and How There Is a Better Way for Africa*. London: Farrar, Straus, and Giroux.

Murray, J. E., A. L. Olmstead, T. D. Logan, J. B. Pritchett, and P. L. Rousseau. 2015. "Roundtable: The Half Has Never Been Told: Slavery and the

Making of American Capitalism. By Edward E. Baptist." *The Journal of Economic History* 75 (3): 919–931.

Nord, Mark, Alisha Coleman-Jensen, Margaret Andrews, and Steven Carlson. 2010. "Household Food Security in the United States, 2009." U.S. Department of Agriculture, Economic Research Service Report No. 108, November.

Nordhaus, William. 2010. "Economic Aspects of Global Warming in a Post-Copenhagen Environment." *PNAS* 107: 11721–11726.

Nordhaus, William. 2013. *The Climate Casino.* New Haven: Yale University Press.

North, Douglas. 1990. *Institutions, Institutional Change, and Economic Performance.* New York: Cambridge University Press.

North, Douglas, John Joseph Wallis, and Barry Weingast. 2012. *Violence and Social Orders.* Cambridge: Cambridge University Press.

Nunn, Nathan. 2008. "Slavery, Inequality, and Economic Development in the Americas." *Institutions and Economic Performance* 15: 148–180.

O'Brien, Patrick. 1988. "The Costs and Benefits of British Imperialism, 1846–1914." *Past and Present* 120: 163–200.

Offer, Avner. 1993. "The British Empire, 1870–1914: A Waste of Money?" *Economic History Review* 46: 215–238.

Olmstead, Alan, and Paul W. Rhode. 2018. "Cotton, Slavery, and the New History of Capitalism." *Explorations in Economic History* 67: 1–17.

Ostrom, Elinor, ed. 2003. *Trust and Reciprocity: Interdisciplinary Lessons from Experimental Research.* New York: Russell Sage.

Piff, Paul K., et al. 2012. "Higher Social Class Predicts Increased Unethical Behavior." *Proceedings of the National Academy of Sciences* 109: 4086–4091.

Pinker, Steven. 2002. *The Blank Slate.* New York: Penguin.

Pogge, Thomas. 2001. "Eradicating Systemic Poverty: Brief for a Global Resources Dividend." *Journal of Human Development* 2: 59–77.

Radin, Margaret Jane. 1989. "Justice and the Market Domain." *Nomos* 31: 165–197.

Rahula, Bhikkhu Basnagoda. 2008. *The Buddha's Teachings on Prosperity.* Wisdom Publications.

Rajan, Raghuram G., and Arvind Subramanian. 2008. "Aid and Growth: What Does the Cross-Country Evidence Really Show?" *Review of Economics and Statistics* 90: 643–665.

Ransom, Roger, and Richard Sutch. 1988. "Capitalists Without Capital: The Burden of Slavery and the Impact of Emancipation." *Agricultural History* 62: 130–166.

Rathbone, Matthew. 2015. "Love, Money and Madness: Money in the Economic Philosophies of Adam Smith and Jean-Jacques Rousseau." *South African Journal of Philosophy* 34: 379–389.

Renwick Monroe, Kristen. 2017. "Biology, Psychology, Ethics, and Politics: An Innate Moral Sense?" In *On Human Nature*, edited by Michael Tibayrenc and Francisco Ayala, 757–770. New York: Academic Press.

Renwick Monroe, Kristen, Adam Martin, and Priyanka Ghosh. 2009. "Politics and an Innate Moral Sense: Scientific Evidence for an Old Theory?" *Political Research Quarterly* 62: 614–634.

Ricardo, David. 1817. *On the Principles of Political Economy and Taxation*. London: John Murray.

Risse, Mathias. 2005. "Does the Global Order Harm the Poor?" *Philosophy and Public Affairs* 33: 349–376.

Roback, Jennifer. 1986. "The Political Economy of Segregation: The Case of Segregated Streetcars." *Journal of Economic History* 56: 893–917.

Rodrik, Dani, Arvind Subramanian, and Francisco Trebbi. 2004. "Institutions Rule: The Primacy of Institutions Over Geography and Integration in Economic Development." *Journal of Economic Growth* 9: 131–165.

Roland, Gérard. 2014. *Development Economics*. New York: Pearson.

Rousseau, Jean-Jacques. 1985. *A Discourse on Inequality*. Reprint ed. New York: Penguin.

Sacerdote, Bruce. 2019. "Fifty Years of Growth in American Consumption, Income, and Wages." NBER Working Paper No. 23292. www.nber.org/papers/w23292.

Sandel, Michael. 2012. *What Money Can't Buy*. New York: Farrar, Straus, and Giroux.

Satz, Debra. 2010. *Why Some Things Should Not Be for Sale*. New York: Oxford University Press.

Schmidtz, David. 2006. *Elements of Justice*. New York: Cambridge University Press.

Schmidtz, David. 2008. *Person, Polis, Planet: Essays in Applied Philosophy*. New York: Oxford University Press.

Schmidtz, David, and Jason Brennan. 2010. *A Brief History of Liberty*. Oxford: Wiley-Blackwell.

Schopenhauer, Arthur. 2004. *The Wisdom of Life*. Mineola: Dover Publications.

Simler, Kevin, and Robin Hanson. 2019. *The Elephant in the Brain*. New York: Oxford University Press, 2018.

Singer, Peter. 1972. "Famine, Affluence, and Morality." *Philosophy and Public Affairs* 1: 229–243.

Singer, Peter. 2010. *The Life You Can Save*. New York: Random House.

Smith, Adam. 1904 [1776]. *An Inquiry Into the Nature and Causes of the Wealth of Nations*. London: Methuen and Co. www.econlib.org/library/Smith/smWN.html#.

Sokoloff, Kenneth L., and Stanley L. Engerman. 2000. "Institutions, Factor Endowments, and Paths of Development in the New World." *Journal of Economic Perspectives* 14: 217–232.

Stern, Nicholas. 2007. *The Economics of Climate Change:The Stern Review*. New York: Cambridge University Press.

Stevenson, Betsey, and Justin Wolfers. 2008. "Economic Growth and Subjective Well-Being: Reassessing the Easterlin Paradox." *Brookings Papers on Economic Activity* 39: 1–102.

Stevenson, Betsey, and Justin Wolfers. 2009. "The Paradox of Declining Female Happiness." *American Economic Journal* 1: 190–255.

Surdam, D. G. 1998. "King Cotton: Monarch or Pretender? The State of the Market for Raw Cotton on the Eve of the American Civil War." *Economic History Review* 55: 113–132.

Sutch, Richard. 1965. "The Profitability of Ante Bellum Slavery—Revisited." *Southern Economic Journal* 31 (April): 365–377.

Svorny, Shirley. 2004. "Licensing Doctors: Do Economists Agree?" *Econ Journal Watch* 1: 279–305.

Tetlock, Philip. 2000. "Coping with Trade-Offs: Psychological Constraints and Political Implications." In *Elements of Reason: Cognition, Choice, and the Bounds of Rationality*, edited by Arthur Lupia, Matthew D. McCubbins, and Samuel L. Popkin. New York: Cambridge University Press.

Tosi, Justin, and Brandon Warmke. 2020. *Moral Grandstanding*. New York: Oxford University Press.

Unger, Peter. 1996. *Living High and Letting Die*. Oxford University Press.

United Nations, Department of Economic and Social Affairs, Population Division. 2015. "World Population Prospects: The 2015 Revision, Key Findings and Advance Tables." Working Paper No. ESA/P/WP.241.

van der Vossen, Bas, and Jason Brennan. 2018. *In Defense of Openness*. New York: Oxford University Press.

Von Neumann, John, and Oskar Morgenstern. 1944. *Theory of Games and Economic Behavior*. Princeton: Princeton University Press.

Weil, David. 2013. *Economic Growth*. 3rd ed. New York: Pearson.

Whaples, R. 1995. "Where Is There Consensus Among American Economic Historians? The Results of a Survey on Forty Propositions." *The Journal of Economic History* 55: 139–154.

Whillans, Ashley, Elizabeth Dunn, Paul Smeets, Rene Bekkers, and Michael Norton. 2017. "Buying Time Promotes Happiness." *PNAS* 32: 8523–8527.

Wright, Gavin. 2006. *Slavery and American Economic Development*. Baton Rouge: LSU Press.

Wright, Robert. 2017. *The Poverty of Slavery*. New York: Palgrave MacMillan.

Wu, Stephen. 2001. "Adapting to Heart Conditions: A Test of the Hedonic Treadmill." *Journal of Health Economics* 20: 495–507.

Zak, Paul, and Stephen Knack. 2001. "Trust and Growth." *Economic Journal* 111: 295–321.

Zelizer, Viviana. 1981. "The Price and Value of Children: The Case of Children's Insurance." *American Journal of Sociology* 86: 1036–1056.

Zelizer, Viviana. 1989. "The Social Meaning of Money: 'Special Moneys'." *American Journal of Sociology* 95: 342–377.

Zelizer, Viviana. 1994. *Pricing the Priceless Child: The Changing Social Value of Children*. New York: Princeton University Press.

Zelizer, Viviana. 1997. *The Social Meaning of Money*. Princeton: Princeton University Press.

Zelizer, Viviana. 2007. *The Purchase of Intimacy*. Princeton: Princeton University Press.

Zelizer, Viviana. 2013. *Economic Lives: How Culture Shapes the Economy*. Princeton: Princeton University Press.

Index

Note: Page numbers in *italics* indicate a figure on the corresponding page.

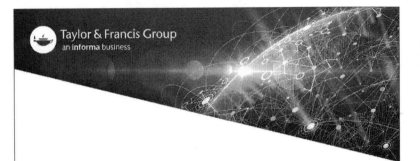